TABLE OF CONTENTS

PROLOGUE

In the beginning I had no idea that my emotional slump and complete lack of motivation were the early signals my mind was giving me that something was wrong. Not only was something wrong in that immediate present, but as time went on there seemed to be no end to the mounting symptoms and increasing discomfort I was experiencing.

For a period of ten years my life was progressively given over to a day-by-day, hour-by-hour effort at coping with a condition whose symptoms can only be described as frightening and bizarre. A condition whose outstanding characteristic is fear, neurotic fear. Fear of space, fear of confinement, fear of travel, fear of groups, and fear of being alone. Then, finally, the fear of fear itself. This, the final fear, which was the fear of experiencing the symptoms of acute anxiety and dread that, for me, filled almost every human undertaking. True fear is never merely psychological. It also has physical concomitants which add to the general unpleasantness; rapidly beating heart, sweaty palms, weak legs, visual confusion, churning stomach. The only remedy for this combination of miseries is to remove yourself from the situation—running away. I came to know all of this intimately. I met these conditions head-on as I lived a life of hiding from my problems, my loved ones, and ultimately hiding from myself.

I was to understand the scope of my psychological deterioration much later and to learn that personal reconstruction is a slow process. It is also a painful encounter with not only the condition of the illness but also a confrontation with the entire scope of personal evolution. In fact, rebuilding the bruised psyche involves more than the efforts of a master builder; it requires an effort at recreation worthy of a diety.

I have been in therapy for about five years at this writing. I am recovering from my fears, from my Agoraphobia, and to some extent I am recovering from the resentment I have felt for the lost years of my life. The time Agoraphobics give to anxiety and fear is lost forever. In fact, even reality is lost during the acute stages of this problem. Because it arises during some of the most productive years of life, careers, marriages, relationships of all kinds suffer from its effects. It produces a personal wasteland from which each individual must try to reclaim himself.

In the succeeding pages, I have tried to present my own case as a personal testament that there is a hope for overcoming the effects of Agoraphobia. I have also included information on the possible causes of the problem, various techniques and methods of treatment, as well as some insight into the direction of current research.

My hope is that my words will reach those who have Agoraphobia and need hope as well as those who understand and want to help.

CHAPTER I

It was very easy at the time to attribute the changes I noted in myself and in my behavior to fatigue, to the onset of middle age, to the weather, or to use any excuse as an explanation to myself and to others for any bit of behavior which seemed out of character. I seemed to be changing from a vital, enthusiastic participant in life to a bored and boring observer. No matter how I tried, I could not feel interest in anything or anyone. My days were spent in merely getting from one hour to the next. I could spend long periods of time looking at the pages of a newspaper or a book and hardly comprehend what I had read. My conversations were contrived pleasantries or hasty remarks which allowed for no response from the listener so that I could make a quick exit from the situation. If the situation were such that I was compelled to remain where I was, I used a drink to fortify myself and to beat down the fear a little. I was losing contacts, friends and for the most part I seemed not to care. Even small duties became horrendous chores which I was sure I would never be able to complete. I alternated between procrastination and a kind of wild activity to get a task over with as fast as possible. I had no idea why I behaved in these ways and the fear I lived with was so dominant that I could not break the cycle long enough to find out what was happening to me.

Yes, there were many signs, many signals from body and mind that all was far from well with me. But instead of responding with concern to the obvious signs of emotional problems and acknowledging that I needed help, I instead became adept at contriving excuses for my behavior. Alibis and excuses were used for the benefit of family, friends and, most of all, myself. I was aware of some secret need to believe that my symptoms would pass. They were too urgent to be ignored and, at the same time, they were too frightening to investigate. I wanted to buy time in the absurd belief that time was on my side. As I reflect on the situation as it was then, my self-delusion seems all the more incredible since all my life I had pursued an academic interest in the field of psychology. I had attained a graduate degree and had made a point of keeping up on current trends in the field, still I did not feel the sense of helplessness that can lead to therapy until some time had passed, and I was indeed helpless. Instead, in the early days of my illness, I fell into the trap of foolish pride and assured myself that if my problems did not spontaneously disappear, I would surely, with my greater understanding, be able to solve them alone. This was not only foolish thinking but it also delayed treatment until it became a psychological emergency, and there was no turning back by then.

This is how it all began. At first my most obvious change in behavior consisted of a general apathy, a lack of enthusiasm, a personal hibernation. In addition to the psychological changes, I experienced a lessening of my physical activities. I no longer had the energy my work needed and the thought of putting forth any recreational effort was out of the question.

It was on my job that the first ominous physical sign showed itself. I was working as a real estate salesperson. I had taken a client to see some country property. When we got to the acreage and I stopped my car, I suddenly realized that I was afraid to open the car door for myself. I hesitated, waiting for the strange feeling of fear to pass and was finally

4

able to leave the car and walk a few yards with my client. I was fortunate in that he was a rancher and preferred to check out the land alone with a map to guide him. He left me alone at the car and this afforded me an opportunity to try to recover my equilibrium and to wonder what had produced the sudden feelings of dread and fear in me. The most baffling aspect of the whole thing as I thought about it was that there was nothing new in the situation, nothing different from countless other times I had shown land to a prospect. As the feeling subsided and we returned to my office, I decided that the whole episode was due to fatigue and tried to put it out of my mind. Real estate is the kind of business that demands a great deal of personal input. That is, not only is it necessary to expend physical energy in the course of making contacts, listing and showing property, dealing in financial, tax and title areas, but energy is also required for the type of personal commitment that is needed for selling. Intellectual and emotional energy are expended almost continuously since real estate agents are always "on call" and available to their clients.

It was in the area of personal commitment that I began to be aware of the symptoms of lessening energy and motivation. I found excuses for longer lunch breaks and reasons to arrive at the office late, if at all. Increasingly I found myself irritated at the complications or delays in some transaction I was working on. Normally delays and red tape are assumed to be an integral part of the real estate business and are seldom taken seriously as they eventually resolve themselves. However, for me, these things were now assuming enormous proportions and each task drained my energies more and more. Some workdays were spent merely sitting in the office, on the telephone, and trying to look busy. As time went by, the less I did, the more enervated I felt. My interest in competing in the marketplace was certainly diminishing and I did not seem to care that it was happening. I did more things mechanically and left many things undone.

A day came when I was routinely showing a home.

5

After I had unlocked the front door and ushered the clients into the living room, I found that I was unable to follow them through the house. In fact, I seemed unable to move at all. It recalled the incident at my car in the country and all the fears came flooding back on me. Several things happened all at once; I felt weak, particularly in my legs, my heart rate increased, my palms became wet, and what I could control of my thoughts told me to get away from the situation as fast as possible. This episode was my first all-out attack of anxiety and panic. It conditioned me to a set of responses that I subsequently had to live with to an ever-increasing extent for the next period of years. I became a slave to fear and the fear grew each time it emerged and it generalized to every aspect of my life from shopping to sex. Fear is more than anxiety. The experience of anxiety is familiar to everyone. Under most circumstances, the amount of anxiety felt at any given time is appropriate to the circumstances which caused it. It is considered normal to feel a combination of apprehension and excitement in new circumstances, during times of change, as in a marriage or a death. In fact, some authorities suggest that a certain amount of anxiety is necessary for a good performance, whatever the task. As is true of any aspect of human behavior, anxiety can vary in both quality and quantity. It is when anxiety is present in extreme amounts and at an inappropriate time that it becomes part of an unhealthy emotional state and is then referred to as neurotic anxiety. I was indeed at this stage of anxiety, although at the time of my first attack, I did not consider the finer distinctions involved in the definitions. The feelings did subside after a time and when I was back in my office again and alone, I began to examine my behavior both out of curiosity and out of fear. Part of my concern was the question again of what was there in the circumstance of showing property that could provoke sudden fear and anxiety in me? Consider the strangeness of the situation; waves of fear and panic arise from no apparent cause and become so strong as to be overwhelming. Normal human functions such as walking, talking, and laughing all seem to demand extra human effort if they are accomplished at all. Suddenly, familiar surroundings are places of dread. People, long known and trusted, provoke fear and the primary motivation is to get away to a safe place, a place where past experience has proven all or most of the symptoms disappear, and to avoid the horrors of mounting anxiety. There is no way to confront these feelings logically since there is no rationale for their presence. The human mind always looks for an explanation and when there is none, the temptation is to fall back on what is known and to construct answers to fit situations whether the logic fits or not.

In addition to the incredible fears I was experiencing, the thought crossed my mind that I might not be able to continue with my real estate work. There is no way in which the real estate business can be conducted without the direct participation of the agent. I was becoming afraid that I would be fearful and anxious every time I had to show property. The fear of having that anxiety state appear came to have a life of its own whenever I allowed myself to think about future situations involving my work. I dreaded going to the office each day and would use any excuse to avoid leaving my home, my safe place. Increasingly my share of the business was being taken over by my partner as I offered excuses of illness or previous appointments. In truth, I was ill but I had no idea of the scope or intensity of that illness at the time.

Several new symptoms began to develop simultaneously as I tried to continue showing properties. As before, I got my clients into my car, drove to the property, and when we had arrived I could barely move out of the driver's seat. It was only with great effort and intense embarrassment that I managed this simple chore. When showing homes, once the front door was unlocked, I was confronted with the problem of feelings of confinement, even in an empty house. I became adept at developing systems of disguise for my true feelings. I would leave the front door ajar, or busy

7

myself raising windows or opening drapes...anything to keep my mind and body occupied. There were often difficult moments when it became necessary to point out a feature in a room or answer a specific question. At these times, my effort at concentration seemed enormous. In spite of the fact that I knew my business well, there were times when my anxiety state became so great that it was an effort of will to respond intelligently to a simple question. When anxiety is present to such a pronounced degree, any external stimulus becomes secondary to the internal stimulus of the anxiety itself. The presence of great anxiety causes the mind and body to focus on how it feels rather than giving attention to anything happening in the environment. Because of this fact, I could barely give my attention to what was happening around me. Yet I am sure, to the casual observer, there was no sign of change in me, although internally I was in a state of extreme discomfort. The most prominent feeling during these times was a desire, or rather a need, to leave the situation at once. The need for flight was accompanied by the physical symptoms of anxiety mentioned earlier. It is not essential for all the symptoms to be present for the pain of anxiety to be felt. Rapid heart, weak legs, sweaty palms, blurred vision and churning stomach can occur in any combination or alone and still be experienced as anxiety. Add to the situation the extreme emotions of fear and panic and there is no doubt how disturbing the experience can be.

Each time that I returned to my office having had any of these feelings recur, I sensed a dread of my next appointment to show property. Without willing it, I now began to take a critical step down the road of my illness; I began to define my world in terms of smaller parameters. I wanted to have more control so I decided to let go of any expansion in my attempts to overcome the problem in any larger sense and to concentrate on controlling those things which I thought were obvious to me. In the case of my work, I observed that showing acreage or any vacant land seemed to produce the most acute symptoms. It seemed that when

I left my car to step off some boundaries, or to point out a view, there was suddenly nothing for me to hang onto or to lean against for support if the weak legs of anxiety appeared. At least when showing a home or a business, there were walls to lean against. Considering all this as a practical analysis of the situation, I arranged with my partner that she would show all the vacant land. I did not mention my real reasons for desiring this change. I merely said that I wanted to specialize in residentials. I was becoming more and more expert at these face-saving excuses. Concurrent with this change in my work habits, I was beginning to limit my social life, too. Whatever was causing the anxiety attacks, I was now beginning to have them in situations and places that I had always felt comfortable in before. I found it increasingly difficult to go out to dinner with people I had known for years. As soon as we were seated at a table in a restaurant, I would begin to feel incredible waves of anxiety. I found myself unable to sit still and I repeatedly changed my position in the chair. I could not keep my mind on the conversation and, in fact, found it difficult to focus my attention on anything except my own internal agony. I had vague flashes of losing complete control of myself in public. This added to the terror and the more I tried to reason with myself, to tell myself to be calm and enjoy the event, the more emotional I became until I was sure there was something wrong with me physically or psychologically or both.

One incident remains clear in my memory because it seemed to embody all of the horrors possible for me to endure at any one time.

It was an early Fall evening and we had made a dinner reservation for four at a fashionable restaurant in the area. It was to be a double celebration—a friend's birthday and the completion of a particularly difficult, but financially rewarding, escrow for me. As soon as we entered the dining room, I was aware of a surge of heat throughout my body and felt my palms and upper lip begin to perspire. (I did not know at the time that these reactions would become painfully familiar to me as time went on.) The room itself was large and quite formal. We were seated somewhere in the center section, under a magnificent chandelier. I recall thinking how dreadful it would be should it fall on me, and at the same time, because I was beginning to feel so anxious, I wished the thing would fall on me. At least then I wouldn't have to sit through dinner. We ordered drinks and I told myself that a cocktail would settle me down. After being served, I drank it down as though it were the last liquid on earth. I was still tense and anxious and could not concentrate on the table conversation. I decided to study the decor, but I noticed that the mixture of lighted chandeliers and brilliant velvet-backed chairs began to swim together as I looked from one to the other. Surely one drink couldn't have that effect on me. I was experiencing another classic anxiety symptom; visual disturbance. By now the dinner orders had been given and the soup had arrived. I stared at it as though it were the enemy ready to rise from the bowl and attack me. There was no way that I felt I could eat at all, much less lift a soup spoon with a steady hand. I was being overwhelmed by myself out of control. I was embarrassed and frightened. I could feel my eyes want to tear and I became desperate to leave the restaurant. Let the chandelier fall into the soup, I *had* to leave. And I did just that, but not without some contrived excuse that I was suddenly not feeling well and needed air. It was a hackneyed explanation but at the time I was in no position to think of anything more original. My companions were concerned but were quick to accompany me to the car. My relief was as sudden as the attack of anxiety had been when we entered the restaurant.

There were other times when the panic took over so completely I had to hastily leave the situation, making vague excuses to old friends. Tears would flood my eyes as I made an awkward retreat from a restaurant or a theater or a party situation. I was helpless and furious at myself at the same time because I couldn't control my feelings. Sometimes I simply refused invitations. This refusal added guilt to my other feelings. I found that even those things I planned myself, I was subsequently withdrawing from with lame excuses. My entire life seemed to center around how I could avoid business or social appointments convincingly.

What was happening to me as far as the expansion of my symptoms into all aspects of my life involved a basic principle of learning called generalization. Generalization takes place when the response made to one stimulus is subsequently made to another stimulus which may or may not be anything like the original stimulus. In my case I had gone from the symptoms originating in my work situation to their appearance also at social situations where there seemed to be no similarity in conditions. At the time this was happening, I did not stop to put events into any kind of neat, logical system. Instead I tried to find a way to deal with symptoms and behavior which were becoming the dominant feature of my life. I was in an adversarial position with myself. It worked in this way: As my symptoms became more extreme and as they appeared more frequently, I just as strongly tried to convince myself that they were of no significance and would soon disappear. Those closest to me tried to talk with me about my obvious discomfort, but I could not face the subject without dissolving into tears. Time and time again, I would put myself into a position of promising to attend an event or travel someplace and as the time for making good on my promises came near, I was overwhelmed by anxiety symptoms. Just before the event, I could not sleep and I found myself going over a litany of "what ifs." What if the car breaks down on a deserted road? What if I faint at the party? What if someone asks me about my behavior? This type of speculation about future events was a hallmark of my general anxiety. The fact that I was constantly preoccupied with possible terrible events in some future meant that I was doing a poor job of dealing with the present. I was inattentive, restless and anxious for things to be over. I felt as though I was always

11

preparing for something that was never finished. There seemed, at the same time, a pressure to get things done. Each day I wanted to come to an end, so that I could just rest. A surge of fatigue would come over me and I wanted to close my eyes and retreat from everything around me.

There were paradoxes at those times which now seem incredible. For example, thoughout the period of my developing symptoms and what I considered strange behavior on my part, others have told me since that most times I appeared completely normal. There were exceptions, such as last minute excuses for not meeting social obligations, or too frequent unexplained "illness." But, in general, I maintained a facade of normalcy. I am sure that the effort expended to achieve this deception was as much for my own benefit as for any other reason. There were many times, when giving in to introspection, that I was sure I was losing my senses. That possibility was more than an idle thought. Allowing myself to consider this possibility was a trap. If I acknowledged something was wrong to myself, I would have to discover what it was, and that discovery could validate my worst fears that, indeed, something was wrong. Acknowledging a disturbance of the psyche is a risky business even in this enlightened age. There are those who do not want to know; there are those who know but want to talk about something more pleasant; and there are those who have made a life career of concern for their own inner life and want to exchange symptoms with you. If I had been developing a physical illness with symptoms obvious to everyone; if I could have pointed to a part of my body and discussed its malfunction, there would have been some consolation in being able to communicate with others. But my developing illness was psychological and only I could experience the symptoms. It seemed to me impossible that anyone could understand what I was suffering. So, for a very long time, I kept my agonies to myself. I developed the art of bluffing and for my own self-perservation, I denied the seriousness of what I was experiencing and got up each

12

day hoping that none of the wretched symptoms would recur.

It is hard, even now, to recall how long this state of mind and body continued—weeks, months, even years of a kind of half-life with my symptoms of fear, anxiety, and depression all merged into one constant misery. As time went on and things did not get better, I was forced to admit that I could no longer work at my real estate office. My apprehension at seeing clients was becoming noticeable and I simply could not keep my mind on my job. After I finally stopped working, I found that I was increasingly depressed and over time, I withdrew from any social contacts at all. This was a hideous time when my contact with reality was tenuous at best. I hated life, my feelings, and whatever inexplicable force had taken over my mind and body. The entire set of symptoms became more intense. I seemed to fear being anywhere except in the safe confines of my own home. Simple routine things such as getting the paper from the front yard were major traumatic events for me. On days when I had to go to the supermarket, I would wake up in the morning with an intense feeling of dread which was unfocused. I realized that I had to go out in the real world and shop for food. This realization caused great panic for me. I became instantly warm and perspiring. My stomach would churn. My mind would alternate between excuses for waiting another day and the frustration of not being able to control my own feelings. The human organism is marvelously inventive when threatened and I felt completely helpless in the face of my overwhelming fears. I invented illnesses which meant someone else would do my shopping. When this excuse was overused, I devised a system of going through a grocery store in a blind rush, literally grabbing those items I needed and racing to the checkstand which had the shortest line. Sometimes just writing a check for my purchases required all the control I could muster. As I waited in the line, every instinct told me to run out of the store, to get away from this place of terror. When at last I was through the line and the check was written and I was safely home, I was completely drained of both mental and physical energy. Each time it happened, I felt I could never go through the experience again. But shopping for groceries was only a minor part of my now fully developed neurosis.

Even in my most self-deceptive moments, I knew I was no longer in control of my life. It was now impossible for me to carry out the day-to-day activities of normal living. I had surrendered to my own personal illness and had finally quit fighting it. Now I began to experience new psychological terrors. I felt guilty; I felt helpless; and I felt alone. The guilt I experienced was mixed with embarrassment each time I had to face someone, even those closest to me, and find that I was unable to offer any objective reason for my misery. My life now seemed to consist of a twenty-four hour crisis situation which I was certain was my own fault somehow, if I could only understand it. I *was* guilty and I felt guilty. But guilty of what? I hadn't contrived the symptoms I was suffering from. I could see no real gain in wanting to continue the awful pain of depression and fear. I was beginning to feel like I should apologize for myself, that I had somehow failed as a human being. I was no longer a functioning, contributing member of society.

Non-performance in today's active, participating society evokes guilt feelings especially if there is no obvious reason for the behavior. A person who is legitimately ill or injured is tolerated only so long as he makes an effort toward normalization. Let him extend his incapacity beyond what is considered standard for his illness, and he becomes any easy target for criticism and the recommendation that he "snap out of it."

I said I felt helpless; but for some reason, I was unwilling to seek the kind of professional help I needed. In some way, I may have felt unconvinced of the enormity of my problems. However, I did look for help in the conventional sense of making an agonizing visit to my physician. After a brief examination and some questions, he prescribed the great medical panacea, tranquilizers. My little call for help was answered with the adult pacifier. Tranquilizers did not help me. Although they softened the onslaught of reality a bit, they did little to alter my inner anxieties. I found, in fact, that a good drink or two did more for my state than any medication. This fact could have been an excuse to use alcohol as the solution for my problems, but I did not want to add that additional difficulty to my repertoire.

Much has been said about the abuse of tranquilizers by patients who take them and by the physicians who prescribe them casually. It seems unfortunate that the most readily available nostrum for the ills of mankind dulls the senses and distorts reality. Since I was having my own problems with reality, anything which distorted my perceptions further was not welcome. At the time of my visit to my physician, I attempted to outline some of my symptoms for him to suggest that there were uncomfortable physical aspects to my psychological problems. I was given my prescription for the tranquilizers and as I left, I had the distinct impression that I had presented to him the picture of the everyday, middle-aged, menopausal female, who needed merely a pat on the head, a good tranquilizer, and a little tincture of time. My helpless feeling was in no way alleviated by this experience and I felt more alone than ever. Since I really could not (or did not) turn to anyone, I was, in fact, alone. Some aspects of this feeling were terrifying. I really felt apart from all the other humans in the world. I felt abandoned. I could not communicate the most important aspects of myself to anyone. I felt a kind of sorrow for my inability to share my feelings. Sorrow for myself and sorrow for the very strong feelings that would never be shared, I tried many times to converse inwardly with myself. I struggled with the appropriate words and syntax. I reasoned that if I could somehow get my thoughts into sequence, maybe I could share them and thereby feel less alone. I was never able to achieve this. What I felt remained at the feeling level and I was alone with it.

Obviously, as I was making no progress in reaching others, as time went on, others no longer sought me out. Not working and having little social life, I had ample time to consider my condition. When I did examine things at all objectively, my first reaction was to hate what I had become—fearful, withdrawn, passive, morbid even. All systems were negative. How could I break the sequence?

As often happens, circumstances force action and I was about to be placed into a position where I would have to perform. There was no alternative.

I have mentioned earlier that among the configuration of symptoms I developed was an inability to travel any distance from my home. Since this was the case, even the popular Sunday drive was now impossible for me to endure. If I did make the effort to go out, I was completely fearful and utterly miserable until I returned home. Any thought of stopping somewhere along the way was out of the question for me. I was too overwhelmed by my anxiety. I used every device I knew to try to overcome the dread of being away from the safety of home. However, since nothing was successful for me, I avoided commitments involving driving altogether. This decision served to isolate me more than ever. I became a prisoner of my own home. Of all the elements of the syndrome which made up my problem, I believe the inability to travel was the most personally frustrating and caused me the most embarrassment. I simply could find no good answers to questions of why I took no weekend trips, no vacations, not even a relaxing drive. I came to dread weekends because they often meant travel invitations which I had to refuse, or if I accepted, I placed myself in the most intensely uncomfortable circumstances. I became truly physically ill from the tension and anxiety associated with forcing myself to make an effort at traveling. The physical discomfort added to my embarrassment and compounded my anxiety.

Another element that seemed to be most disabling

was my fear of confined places such as theaters, restaurants, and offices. It may seem paradoxical that it is possible for a person to show fear of open spaces and a fear of small, closed places at the same time. But the nature of the illness is such that this paradox can easily prevail. Because I had no understanding of my illness at the time, I foolishly allowed myself to be put in the position where my two worst fears—travel and confinement—were combined. I had purchased season tickets to the San Francisco Opera and since attending meant a car trip of some 230 miles from my home, I was set up for a test of my strongest fears. My companion and I left the morning of the performance, and I managed the trip somehow. I was most desirous of attending the opera and my excitement at the prospect was in a struggle with my mounting nervousness as we got further and further from the safety of home.

We arrived at the opera house about one hour before the performance was to begin, and we had drinks and a luncheon in the house's restaurant. Attempting to describe my feelings during this time is something like trying to re-form the ingredients taken from a blender. There were so many emotions all at once; the excitement of the event itself, the ambience of one of the world's great opera houses, being in a crowd, the realization that home was too far away to run to, and not the least, a need to prove to myself and to others that I was in control of myself and my reactions. Mine was the best performance of the day. Once seated and the house lights out, I felt some easing of the tension and I tried to enter into the performance on the stage. If I allowed my thoughts to return to myself and where I was, the familiar waves of panic would return. It took a mighty effort of will to remain seated at those times. I was restless in my seat, constantly adjusting my posture and rolling and unrolling my program. By bracing my back hard against my seat and somehow pressing my feet and knees against the seat in front of me, I was able to keep myself seated and somewhat in control. I managed to make it through a couple of operas, but as I mentioned, I had *season* tickets. With several performances to see, I was trying various techniques to help me cope with the anxiety and fear. On two occasions I stayed at a motel the night before the performance. This strategy proved to be a mistake. The confinement in a motel room was worse than the early morning car trip. On one occasion, I sat through the performance until the last act. At that point, I became absolutely terrified that if I did not leave at once, something dreadful would happen to me. The panic was in my legs, in my throat, and I felt compelled to run up the aisle and out. It was an embarrassing, frustrating, and miserable experience. I was in tears by the time I reached the car and my companion was furious with me, and justifiably so. It became very obvious that I was not winning the battle for control. The drama of this situation cannot be exaggerated. It was an internal war of the kind that can demonstrate the resiliency of the human spirit. Even up to the last minutes before leaving the opera house, I had tried to convince myself that I would make it; that I had conquered my personal demon. It would never be that easy, as I found out later.

After this episode, I no longer tried to attend the opera. My last facade of normalcy had been pulled away and I allowed the fear and apathy to take over. I went nowhere, saw very few people, and then mostly in my own home. I began to settle into my neurosis. Still I did nothing about seeking professional help. As it turned out, it was through others who acted on my behalf that I was finally to get help. And this occurred only after my most acute attack of symptoms under the most trying set of circumstances.

My companion had applied to a university in a neighboring state for a year's graduate work and I was to go also. The commitment to a change of residence temporarily was made long before my symptoms became so troublesome. When the notice of acceptance came, I was overwhelmed with mixed feelings. Fear and anxiety (my old friends) were joined with guilt if I did not meet my part of the original bargain. That original bargain was first struck between Marianne and me at a much earlier time when we jointly decided that she would pursue work on her doctorate. I would work in real estate and do most of the homemaking so that she could be free for study and research. It seemed like such a perfect arrangement when we first made our plans. Each of us was looking forward to a new environment and a chance to get back into the university life again. It would be considerably difficult to alter all the carefully made arrangements at such a late date in order to accommodate my problem in traveling. I weighed the idea of remaining at home alone, but in the condition I was in, neither of us thought that would be a good idea. Besides, I needed someone to help me support myself since I was unable to work at all. Marianne was most generous and understanding. She understood my problem as well as anyone not afflicted with it could. But in the end it had to be my decision.

I struggled with conflict for some time and finally made up my mind that I would go also. My part of the bargain meant that I would be responsible for the arrangements, doing the planning as well as the packing. I knew that I had to pace myself so I began the preparations early. In some ways that strategy proved to be a mistake. The collecting of the boxes for packing, sorting what to take and what to store, plus the general disorder of such an undertaking proved to be a constant reminder that I was going to travel; to move. I have since understood that leaving the sanctuary of a safe place can be psychologically tantamount to the worst kind of physical pain.

I was deliberately inflicting the worst possible combination of circumstances on myself. Whenever I allowed myself to think about what I was doing, I would also lapse into a rationale about how it was to be for only one year, that many of my personal belongings were to accompany me, and even the old cliche "it would do me good." My self deception should have been obvious, but as usual I was blind to my own traps.

Time passed and as the date for our departure grew nearer I became more and more apprehensive. Anxiety was now a constant companion. At times I couldn't keep my mind on what I was doing so that I was often unpacking something I had just packed. It seemed to take forever for me to empty a cupboard. Each time I finished packing a box, I was exhausted both psychologically and physically. It was a fortunate thing that I had started the work early because with each day that passed I became more and more confused and fatigued. Finally, one day in desperation I called my physician again for tranquilizers. This time they seemed to help less than before. I was becoming terrified at the prospect of the trip but I was also completely without alternatives. Now anxiety was turning into panic. I could feel it building in myself like some insidious virus. For me the difference between anxiety and panic is the factor of action. Anxiety can be a part of the general psychological environment at any time. When it is too intense and persistent it may overpower rational thought processes and can lead to a change in behavior. But when panic develops out of anxiety there is usually immediate action taken. It is often irrational and can even lead to harm for the person affected. But there is no way to overcome panic except through action. In the case of anxiety, however, it can be and often is borne without any action being taken to relieve it.

Throughout this period of trip preparation, I felt as though I were being abandoned or as though I were disassociating myself from everything I had known. Yet I knew that made no sense since everything dear and close to me was going with me. The feelings were with me hour after hour, day and night, an unrelenting accompaniment to everything I did. I had never felt so miserable in all my life.

At last the day to leave was only a night away. That night was incredible. Since I was wide awake, I used the time to turn over any possibilities for extricating myself from the trap I had set. I envisioned not going at all but that would be impossible both from a practical and a personal perspective.

After all, plans had been made which included me as a necessary part of their completion. There was no option. In the morning I would have to leave my home, get into the car and travel hundreds of miles away. In the ordinary course of events, for the ordinary person, contemplation of such an event would have been exciting. For me, it represented all the horrors of all the nightmares I ever had joined together in a single, all-pervasive fear. When dawn came I was an emotional basket-case. I went through the motions of dressing, breakfast and the last minute collection of personal belongings. I could hardly make intelligent conversation, my emotional state was so extreme.

At last we were in the car and underway. In deference to my strange malady, it was decided to drive straight through to our destination, thus avoiding overnight in a motel. Seventeen hours of continuous driving—an enduro by any standards. As I think back and try to recapture the dominant thoughts and feelings at that time, I can recall a sense of complete alienation, of being cut off forever from all safety. I could no longer worry about an automobile malfunction or the fact that each mile took me further away from home. I was beyond concern for particulars and could only feel a sense of loss of self and a feeling of complete hopelessness. Time, of course, passed along with the miles and eventually we arrived at our destination. It was very late and we were tired. After rousing our landlord, we were shown the house we had arranged for—sight unseen. Emotionally drained by the whole experience, sleep came easily at last.

The house was very old. It both looked and smelled old. It stood on a very large lot almost obscured by bushes and trees. Beyond the trees there were trees. Panic surfaced and I felt I was being imprisoned by those trees. I just could not see beyond them and I felt I could never get out of their grasp. I tried to keep these feelings from rising to the surface and dominating my thoughts. I unpacked and tried to rid the place of the musty, uncared-for smell old houses often retain.

Each time I placed something on a counter or in a cupboard, I fought with my feelings. What was I doing in this unfamiliar place? How could I bear it for an entire year? When alone, I cried with fear as much as anything. The sensation of unreality that is characterisitic of some human situations came over me in that situation. I knew that I could not bear the conditions, so some part of me said that they just did not exist. It was a fantasy, surrealistic, and it would pass. It was as though one part of my psyche was trying to protect the rest of it.

The house was on three levels, bedroom and bath both at the street level; living room, dining and kitchen downstairs; and finally laundry and storage facilities in the basement. If the air in the rest of the house could be described as musty, the air in the basement was decayed. Each time I entered the basement it was with a certainty that it would be my tomb. I felt myself enclosed by that house and imprisoned by those trees surrounding it. And what of my fears, my anxieties; all the symptoms I had grappled with for so long? They grew in intensity each day. I was using every distraction I could think of: I took the tranquilizers, I drank more than usual, I tried to involve myself in reading, in television, in work in that house. But, insidiously, day by day, I knew my feelings were growing out of hand. My fears were more intense and anxiety was part of everything I did or thought. In spite of all this, in an odd, detached way, I marveled at how much emotional strength I seemed to have. I was struggling to survive.

During this time my companion was busy with the adjustments of attending the university and the requisites of academic life. Because of this I found myself alone most days from early morning until late afternoon. This solitary time did nothing to help my condition. I often felt abandoned and lonely in a strange place. My hold on the reality around was perilous. It is an experience without peer to become aware of the deterioration of your own reason and the disintegration of your own spirit, and to further understand that you have no resources to help yourself. There is nothing in human experience so devastating as the loss of control of your life. When a person loses himself what has he left? Everything else becomes void. My psychological unraveling was now extreme and I had no alternative but to give in to my feelings. This capitualtion took the form of telling my companion through copious tears that I could no longer remain away from home; that dramatic and absurd as it seemed I must return and could not fulfill my part of our agreement. One of the more difficult aspects of the problem which I had developed, and which others have experienced too, is the manner in which relationships are affected. I have come to understand that many marriages end in separation or divorce because one spouse, contending with the limitations of Agoraphobia, is unable to fully participate in normal family relationships such as dining out, traveling, and general socializing. But this is knowledge that I acquired much later in this story. What I was feeling at the time, besides guilt for running out on my companion, was remorse for all I had asked her to put up with during the development of my condition. We had been companions and had shared a home together for more than twenty years. After the severity of my problem caused me to stop my real estate work, she was very supportive of my difficulties, although she understood them no better than I did. Together we had put in a year of planning and preparation for the trip and her entrance into the university to complete her doctoral degree. Now, after so short a period of time away from home, I was faced with finding some way to help us both understand what was happening to me. Obviously, the prospect of my leaving was a devastating blow to her. I knew that I was asking for a great deal of sympathy and patience for my plight, while completely ignoring the position I was placing her in. Our long time relationship was important to us both and had she not been such a compassionate friend, I am sure that this unfortunate situation would have been a good reason for her to end the relationship. As it developed the good years together had forged a bond between us which withstood even the most difficult aspects of my illness. I am forever thankful for the good fortune of having such a person to help me through the most destructive time in my life.

The thought uppermost in my mind was how I would be able to transport myself from where I was to where I wanted to be. I was becoming desperate now that the decision to leave had been made. I hated the situation and I loathed myself and my pathological weakness. After some maneuvering, a friend agreed to fly to where I was and then return home with me immediately. Fortunately I had the type of friend who did not probe for details or point out obvious incongruities in my behavior. I could not explain myself to myself, let alone offer any cogent insights for someone who had just arrived on the situation.

The morning I was to return home was one of the strangest times in my life. From someplace I found the strength to get on a plane with my friend and fly away. Strangest of all was the euphoria I felt with the realization that I was leaving that musty house and those strangling trees. I was manic for a while and the anxiety, fatigue and depression were gone. It was a pleasant madness while it lasted. I felt suspended between realities—my familiar reality of tension and pain was now displaced by the false relief I felt at having removed myself from the source of my terrors. My reprieve was shorr lived. Very soon after my return home, all my familiar problems returned.

It was necessary for me to stay with friends which was an unsatisfactory arrangement. I was now pressed on all sides to offer some explanation for my sudden return. Adding to this embarrassement was my growing guilt at having left my companion and my obligations. It took a month of personal soul searching plus a few conferences with a psychiatrist, some strong medication and I was finally ready to attempt the return to my obligations. But not to the same house I had left. In my absence, my companion had been able to find a newer, more open style house which was decidedly more acceptable to my state of mind.

To be able to make the return flight and to conduct myself in a near normal manner, I took many pills. Medication was then my only recourse until I could settle in one place. Besides, I was no longer trying to hide the fact that something was wrong with me, although I still had no satisfactory name for the problem. If the pills would provide the kind of courage I needed, no matter how false, I was willing to take them. So with that help and my own high resolve, I took a return flight to a new start away from home.

During my absence, some arrangements had been made which would further force me to deal with my problems and with myself. When I so abruptly left in my state of near hysteria, I hadn't realized how sick I had appeared to others at the time. I could barely remember how I had behaved except that I had no ability to deal with anything at the time. I recall having one goal and that was to remove myself from an utterly terrifying situation and to return to the safety of my former home. I behaved like the stereotype drowning victim, making one last desperate grasp at anyone or anything that could save him from death. I had managed to save myself but to forestall any further problems, others had arranged for me to enter into therapy. At last I was to meet and to pursue my long-time enemy.

CHAPTER II

Someone once wrote, "I have met the enemy and he is me." There is more truth than bad grammar in that thought. Psychotherapy, in whatever manner it is presented, is first and foremost a confrontation with the self. MOre often than not, that confrontation is painful and lengthy. It can be painful because most of us give our lives over to perfecting our facades, our image that we present to the world. Our interpersonal commerce has been carried on using this disguise and as we mature we usually come to believe in the legitimacy of this mask. Worst of all, we can fool even ourselves as we become convinced that what we have cultivated as our public personality is really who we are. Even a little time in therapy is sufficient to understand that many of those things which ail us psychologically have their origins in not understanding or not accepting the real dimensions of ourselves. We give great time and much effort over to developing our masks and no doubt they serve a purpose in aiding human interchange, but the essential essence of a person can become lost in the process. When this happens the way back for an individual to himself often means meeting himself as enemy and forcing a confrontation. This, too, can be painful. Good therapy helps us to bear the pain and withstand the confrontation.

In my personal confrontation with myself, I soon

learned that I had mistaken my facade for the real thing and in so doing I had allowed the edges of what I felt and thought to become blurred by what I *thought* I should think and feel. One of the fascinating and yet embarrassing aspects of psychotherapy is that often one quickly comes to recognize his own defenses. They may have served him well for a lifetime but once they are seen for the charade they are, there follows a distrust of your own judgment. The inclination is to question "how could I be so trapped by my own devices?" My enemy was me and I was at psychological war with myself. Indications of my war were made known to me by the configuration of symptoms and behavior changes that I had been experiencing for so long. This particular bit of insight was not part of my understanding when I took the giant step into a therapist's office for the first time. In fact there was little that I understood except that I was there at the appointed time. My feelings were somewhere between apprehension and skepticism. Although I had a lifelong interest in psychology and had obtained an advanced degree myself, I was personally unconvinced of any practitioner's ability to effect permanent changes in human behavior. In spite of my bias, I had to admit that I was reduced to the status of victim of my own behavior so I had little to lose by following through on an appointment which had been made in my interest.

It was a warm afternoon in late summer and the interior of the office was cool with subdued lighting. I had been well supplied with tranquilizers and had taken one just before leaving for the appointment. Even so, I was very nervous, not only because I was seeing a new doctor for psychotherapy but also because, as usual, I was in an anxious situation away from the safety of home.

The exchange of greetings was informal and I tried to appear relaxed and in charge of myself. Why I wanted to act in this manner I will never understand since I hadn't possessed those characteristics for months. I was asked to begin with a history of my illness and then go on to a history of my life. This assignment sounds simple enough until you begin trying to relate your private world of horrors to a public system of timekeeping. Did I first notice the symptoms months ago, years ago? I wondered if there was ever a time without them. So I talk about myself, self-consciously, and tried to set things into some sort of time perspective. Yes, it was necessary to impose order and limits even on those aspects of life which were troubling simply because they had no order or limits. Talking sense about the non-sensible was new and difficult for me. I had spent so much time in denial that for me to now formalize what I had tried to ignore was almost impossible. How to tell about the absurd fears that had grown throughout the years to the point which I could no longer leave my home and function in the world of events and places and people. How to tell about the dread of having to spend a moment talking to a neighbor. How to convey the utter terror of the weekends with its friends and dinners, and drives that became agonizing experiences. And the worst part, the deep depression that wakes up with you in the morning and stays around all day, countermanding any intention you might have for action. All these feelings needed words and, imperfect though they were, I found them during this first long session. I found also that there was some relief in the unloading, in sharing the experiences with someone else. How naive we are to assume that our private experiences are somehow unique and impossible of understanding by others. But I had lived with my secrets for so long it was incredible to me that another person was listening to me and was interested in my state of mind. Little by little that afternoon I was able to bring things into focus so that what I had experienced became somewhat intelligible.

In the course of my self-revealing sessions, I gradually became aware of the dominant part my illness had played in my life. I began to understand how everything else had become second to my efforts toward containing my symptoms while pretending to myself and to others that they did not exist. It was great relief to finally develop some perspective on my situation through the eyes of someone else and most of all it was a comfort to know that I was no longer alone in my misery. Probably the greatest service a therapist performs for a client is to affirm for him the fact that he is not alone, that his suffering is understood, and that he is valued for himself, sick as he may be, by at least one other human. For me as a first time patient, these initial strengths which were present in the therapy situation were a lifesaver. I was also fortunate in finding a person with whom I could communicate at the beginning. With guidance I was able to use the healthier part of myself to understand and aid the unhealthy part. It is not always easy to begin and to advance a relationship where one of the parties opens his soul to the other, and in effect, seeks validation of himself through the understanding of a stranger. It takes time to become comfortable in this unique situation as you sort out your life and your problems. I stepped into therapy like an innocent into the water, trusting in some guiding hand to help me stay afloat. I learned in the course of events that I would do much of the guiding myself. I learned to participate in the cure as much as I had participated in the illness.

So we began together, my therapist and I, to talk about my symptoms and their beginnings. I could see that they did conform to a pattern and fit a framework that others had known, and that what I felt was my own unique disorder had indeed been experienced by others. I felt extreme relief at finding this out. It made things easier to bear somehow if I could say I had an illness that had a name.

Agoraphobia. The word comes from the Greek agora, which means a place of assembly, and phobos, which means flight or panic. According to Dr. Claire Weeks, an authority on the subject and a pioneer in treatment techniques, the word agoraphobia was first used to describe the condition in 1871. Throughout the decades since then little information has developed about Agoraphobia except a knowledge of its symptoms. Not only has Agoraphobia been hidden from the experience of the professionals but it has also been hidden from families and friends and, in a sense, from the Agoraphobic himself. In the privacy of their own thoughts, Agoraphobics are terrified of losing their minds or of committing an act of self-destruction. Like many other illnesses, Agoraphobia seems to attack at the prime of adulthood, during years that should be productive and rewarding. Time that could have been used creatively becomes a fear-ridden, moment-by-moment struggle to survive.

Traditional psychiatric or psychological techniques have shown little success in effecting cures. As mentioned earlier, medicine has used tranquilizers and other sedative drugs which have helped little if at all. Because of the peculiar nature of its symptoms which keep the victim from leaving home to seek help, it has been a hidden illness. Those whose condition allowed them to leave their homes for professional help have been fortunate at least in being able to talk with someone about the condition, to bring it out in the open. But in most cases, even today, the Agoraphobic suffers alone, living with miseries which are very much like my own which I have described on these pages.

The history of the understanding and acceptance of Agoraphobia as a disabling illness is very recent. As better methods of controlling its symptoms have developed, more can be done to at least help the Agoraphobic out of some of the ravages of constant fear and anxiety. At present, the most successful method of treatment is a desensitization process whereby the patient is helped to confront his fears and panics by a process of gradual desensitization and conditioning. He is exposed to the feared place or condition while in the presence of an understanding helper and is encouraged to remain in the situation as long as possible, knowing that he can retreat if conditions become too much for him to bear. There are no reprisals for failure. There is praise for any small amount of success. Each successive encounter with the feared situation is gradually increased in time or intensity and by these gradual increments, at his own pace, the Agoraphobic can master his panic and anxiety as he learns to resume a more normal life. This is the general model for behavior modification therapy and has been shown to be more or less successful in overcoming many of the incapacitation aspects of this illness. Because many of those who have Agoraphobia have had it for many years, the expectation of a quick "cure" is unrealistic. However, great progress can be made in eliminating or at least lessening many of the uncomfortable symptoms associated with the illness.

The most difficult aspect of treating Agoraphobia is that it is unique within the category of phobias. In the case of fear of heights, fear of animals, or any other discrete fear, it is usually possible to avoid or ignore whatever produces the phobic reaction without undue disruption of a person's entire life. Agoraphobia, however, is a fear complex which spreads its influence into every aspect of the victim's existence. It is never possible to avoid or ignore its presence. It makes total encroachment into everything, and, in fact, changes the individual as he made accommodations to integrate the phobia and his personality. This important difference which is characteristic of Agoraphobia makes it necessary for the therapist who works with an Agoraphobic to adopt a more eclectic approach in treatment. Instead of treating a person who has a phobia in the traditional sense, treating an Agoraphobic means working with an individual whose entire life and personality turn on his illness. While most Agoraphobics have some symptoms in common, few will have all the symptoms. There are always some discomforts which are unique to the individual. Some people are able to drive their cars but must avoid freeways. Some can leave home but must be accompanied by an understanding companion. Some cannot bear to open their front door.

Where does such an aberration come from? How can it be cured? Do its victims have anything besides their illness in common? Each of these questions is without a definitive answer at this time. Some theories suggest that the development of Agoraphobia is part of a general anxiety state, or a learned reaction to stress. In the case of the stress reaction, it is not only situational stress but also stress that is prolonged over a period of time with no let up. In terms of "cure," the most successful results have come from using the techniques of desensitization as described earlier. In using this technique, it is the symptoms or the behavior which is changed or "cured." While this may bring a feeling of great relief to a victim of Agoraphobia who now finds places and conditions which formerly caused panic or fear no longer provokes these feelings, the underlying causes for the development of the phobic condition may still be present. Treatment with tranquilizer drugs or electroshock therapy have generally been unsatisfactory for long term cures.

Generally speaking, the professional literature on the subject of Agoraphobia is scant, except for the more recent work of the behaviorists and the desensitization programs. For countless sufferers, the existence of Agoraphobia as a recognized illness is news. In most cases, the illness is believed to be a personal burden, borne alone and in obscurity. This is the pathetic paradox of Agoraphobia: its victims need help but because of the nature of their problem they cannot even try to obtain help.

All this and more I came to appreciate and to understand through several years of professional help along with countless hours of reflection and introspection and study. Out of this experience I have gained some practical skills for coping with my symptoms. I have also increased my knowledge of the turns of fate which led me to develop such a debilitating problem. From this personal perspective and from contact with other Agoraphobics, I have developed my own theoretical position regarding the three questions posed earlier: origin, cure and characteristics of the Agoraphobic. More of this later—for now it is important to return to the beginnings of my own therapy and to its contributions to my present development.

As a beginning patient in therapy, I was probably not

the most congenial or receptive person to work with. I was only marginally convinced that I would achieve any real results from the situation and my motivations for going at all were strictly as a last resort and to appease family and friends. I had more or less bought the idea that things were hopeless for me. I was convinced that no amount of rehashing my life could lead anywhere. Added to this attitude was an underlying feeling of some embarrassment concerning certain aspects of my life and a real reluctance to bring forth old ghosts. It turned out that none of these feelings were unique in the experience of the therapist. As Freud himself once said, "Nothing human is foreign to me." No doubt every therapist agrees with Freud on at least this point.

My initial visits were tense and intensive. They ranged from two to three hours in duration and took place once a week. This technique of long sessions was described by the therapist as allowing for more concentration and closer follow-through on whatever material might develop during a session. From the patient's view, it seems to be an exhausting time both emotionally and physically. However, it did allow for point-by-point probing without the necessity of clock watching. It is still amazing to me how much personal material which I believed had been buried under layers of time, rationalization and plain old forgetting began to surface. Almost in surprise I found myself revealing bits and pieces of information about myself, my life and my feelings which seemed to come from an inventory of experiences I had forgotten I'd had. At times I felt like an audience and at the same time I felt like the speaker. I listened to my own words as though they were spoken by someone else. Over time I became more at ease in the situation as I felt that the therapist's office was a "safe place" for me to be. After about six months I was able to drive myself to my appointments— a giant leap. This small achievement was a milestone for me as I had done little driving alone since I had quit the real estate business so long ago.

My therapist was always very encouraging when I relayed my latest triumph to her. I was exceedingly fortunate in have a knowledgeable and caring therapist as my first introduction to the therapy process. She was a very tall, large woman in her late thirties and would be characterized as a 'handsome' woman. Among my first impressions, I noted her eyes. They were intense and fixed completely on the person across from her. Many times I had difficulty meeting that concentrated look but knowing it was there gave me a good feeling. She seemed really to care about my difficulties and to go a step beyond the professional requirements of our relationship. Therapists as individuals are as different as anyone else but taken as a group, they seem to possess a special human quality that has nothing to do with their education, training or economic status. It would become nearly impossible to effect a good relationship between such strangers if a rapport was not established early on. In the therapy process this rapport is critical. Dr. S. and I established a very positive working relationship and when I had to leave after a year under her care, I knew I had had a unique experience.

Part of my therapy with Dr. S. consisted of "assignments" each week to be completed by the next session. The "assignments" meant that I was to go with my companion to a shop, grocery store, or a restaurent, and practice staying in the situation without panic as long as possible. Sometimes I would set a time goal such as ten minutes in the drugstore. By using an interval of time which I pre-set, I was able to control the situation myself. Sometimes I would go to a shop with a specific item in mind, and I would look for the item, buy it, and leave. All of this practicing in the real world was the practical application of behavior modification therapy. As pointed out earlier, this technique is usually effective in gradually changing behavior. It makes use of the principles of learning combined with concern and praise from an interested friend or a therapist. The point in changing the behavior is to help restore the patient's confidence and provide him with the means of getting along in the world in a more or less normal manner. None of this process was easy and often I would fail to carry out an assignment because of too much anxiety in the situation or even too much anxiety just thinking about it. On those occasions when I was successful, however, I felt triumphant and relieved that I was meeting the "enemy" head on. But often the good feelings would give way to the bad when I tried to extend my accomplishments further and do more than I was ready for. I was so anxious to have the whole thing behind me, it was difficult to be patient and accept things in small doses.

Each week as I went to my therapy sessions, I reported on how the assignment had gone. So as not to rely on my memory alone, I also kept a daily journal both as a chart of progress and as a diary of my feelings from day to day. It was tedious and part of me rebelled at documenting thoughts and feelings for another to read.

Early in the therapy I experienced two types of feelings relative to the whole process: I was in awe of the positive change in feeling that came with each session but I was also resentful of the fact that I was letting go of something of myself to another. It was as though it were a type of enforced sharing that seemed to leave me barren. Consequently, there were times when I held back and did not allow thoughts and feelings to flow as freely as they might have. It is true that personal vanity or even timidity can interfere with therapy even though the situation is supposed to be working in your own best interests. The singularity of the therapy situation produces surprising responses that are not present in any other human exchange. In any other relationship, it could be advantageous to bend the truth a little, to exaggerate for effect; to lie. But to apply this type of behavior in the therapy situation is absurd and self-defeating. In most cases this fact becomes obvious and, consequently, masks tend to come off and lies dissolve. For once, truth is confronted and weaknesses are appraised. Buried feelings and needs surface. Even the most intimate relationships do not produce the healing candor that can come within the therapy situation. As I gained more time and experience I was less surprised at the myriad of mixed feelings the process brings about.

By using the journal and the assignments, two things were happening: I was getting actual experience in coping with my world of frightening situations and I was developing a day by day chronicle of my inner feelings relative to the experiences and to anything else I thought might be important. The system also served as a guide for the therapist during each session. The early assignments took a great deal of courage to execute. Deliberately placing yourself in the path of fear and panic is difficult no matter how great the satisfaction of accomplishment is later. On several occasions, I found myself hurrying through the situation so that I could have it over with and could report to my therapist that I had completed the assignment. It seemed that my desire was to please the therapist rather than to get any value from the experience myself. One assignment was particularly noteworthy because it showed me again how powerful Agoraphobic reactions can be. It also pointed out how necessary it is to have great confidence in your therapist.

It was decided after a few months of therapy that I should try my new coping tools on my worst nemesis: traveling overnight and staying in a motel. The journey was carefully planned. My therapist had made it many times and so tried to prepare me for various things along the way. We discussed the distance between small towns, where a good restaurant was located, and the time between leaving home and returning the next day. It was a journey of about one hundred miles. I had my therapist's phone number and was instructed to call any time I felt I was in trouble.

Calling my therapist between appointments was a very difficult thing for me to do. Among the many prohibitions of my childhood was that you should not be a nuisance to your doctor, because he is busy. What I came to understand later was that it was part of Dr. S.'s procedure to make telephone contact with her patients between office visits. I often wondered how she found the time and energy for this additional work. But I must concede that the fact that she showed this extra concern was very heartening to me.

As the time to leave grew closer, I began to experience all the old symptoms of apprehension and dread I had experienced when we left on our original trip. I tried to use some of the techniques I had learned to drive the fear down to a manageable level. I used deep breathing exercises to help my body relax. I tried to think of the shortness of the time and distance, and how pleased I would feel if I could carry out this most difficult assignment. I knew that I could turn back if I needed to but I tried to put that fact out of my mind. I knew that I would feel guilty if I couldn't make it. Each failure that I experienced caused me to have a period of deep depression during which I loathed myself and the world around me. I was determined not to have that feeling again.

The appointed day arrived and we drove off in the early afternoon. I noted the time with great anxiety as I realized that I would not see my home again for twenty-four hours. I was near tears and tried to focus my attention on the cars or the passing landscape. As I was staring out the car window, my mind was racing ahead of me, concerned with all the "what-ifs" I could conjure up. What if the car broke down; what if I got sick; what if we became lost? It was an endless series of absurd concerns. I struggled with my thoughts as my stomach grew tighter and my knees weaker with each passing mile. I alternated between "I can't make it" and "I've got to make it." Finally we arrived at the restaurant the therapist suggested we stop at. We drove around the block several times while I surveyed the situation. At last I had to admit to my companion that I just could not stop there. The whole idea of walking into a strange place with the high anxiety I was feeling was just out of the question. We drove on.

We arrived at the motel, a beautiful location on the Pacific Ocean. We obtained the room key and noted that there was a bar and restaurant as part of the motel complex. We went into the bar while I hoped a drink would bolster my courage. As usual the alcohol did lower my anxiety and we finally ordered something to eat. Fortunately for me the restaurant had few customers at that time and so I managed to survive the meal. Another hurdle passed, but time was crawling. As soon as we left the restaurant I experienced the sinking feeling that told me I was in trouble. Suddenly the thought of returning to that motel room filled me with dread again. But I couldn't keep walking around either so the obvious alternative was to return to the room.

After being in the room for some minutes, I began to take inventory of my feelings. My most pervasive feeling was that I was confined to my room against my will. The room was alien and threatening to me. To distract myself from these thoughts I turned on the television, took a shower and tried to make friends with the situation. In reality the only thing I could think of doing was running away from the situation. I was very disappointed in myself because I knew I was failing again. All my feelings came in waves like nausea and had the effect of making me feel tearful and weak. I realized that when I was away from home I was always aware of myself, of my bodily feelings. On the other hand, when I was at home or in a safe place I was able to concentrate on things other than myself.

We had arrived at the motel in the early afternoon. It was now near nine in the evening and it was obvious to both my companion and me that I would not be able to stay the night. So we checked out of the motel and drove into a fast-forming fog. There were no recriminations from my companion about the necessity of leaving, but there was some concern about the advisability of driving in the fog at such a late hour. However, in spite of the late hour, the bad weather and the fact that we were both very tired, we headed the car toward home. Where minutes before I had been swamped by my feelings of fear, I was now delighted to be going home. My enemy had won again, but I could feel only relief because I didn't have to endure a miserable experience.

As we were driving along a particularly curving road, with poor visibility due to the fog, suddenly our car lights went out—a frightening experience. Moving to high beams restored the lights but I couldn't help but notice the difference between fear an external incident provoked and the type of fear I had lived with which was caused by my own internal processes. In the case of the "real" fear, I was able to function, to think: where is the flashlight?; do we have flares? Internal fear had always led only to flight from the situation in panic.

As I said earlier, not only did this incident of leaving the motel point out how strong an Agoraphobic reaction can be in motivating behavior, it also illustrated for me how important it is to have confidence in the therapist. At the time of this venture I did not have that confidence built up. I had merely followed my own instincts, returned to my home, and was willing to accept and forget the incident as one more failure. My therapist had a different view. Early the following morning my phone rang and I was told by my therapist how wrong I was in not telephoning when I was first in trouble at the motel. Didn't I understand that the therapist was there for help and reinforcement? In truth, at that point, I did not fully understand. Too many years of trying to handle the situation alone had made me unprepared for another's interest and help. So I had been a bad patient in this situation. It was some time before I no longer felt guilty about the entire incident, but my therapy went along from there.

The therapy process is somewhat like a personal religious experience. There must be a commitment made to the process and to the person involved in it. It does no good to offer token homage or to hold reservations if any positive return is expected for the time and money invested. It often takes time for a totally efficient relationship to develop and if it does not evolve naturally from the situation, it is better to change therapists than to force a fit that is not there. No therapist is an oracle but some are more capable than others in directing thinking and/or behavior which results in the insights necessary to make a difference for the patient.

Under the guidance of my first therapist I did begin to gain some insight into those things in my life which could have contributed to my developing something as disabling as Agoraphobia. Mostly, however, I learned to change my behavior and to move from a half-life to an awkward attempt at normalcy. That is, I learned how to cope with some of the symptoms my illness produced and I learned not to panic whenever the symptoms arose. The system of behavior modification seems simple in the telling and perhaps it is, but by using its methods under guidance, I was helped at a time in my life when the condition had become so acute that it was indeed life-threatening. Had I not been able to see some possibility of improvement in my condition, I would have preferred death to the pseudo-life I had been living for so long.

In recapping the events of my initial year of therapy, it is fair to say that a tourniquet was applied to the wound and I was able to function, but the pathology was still present and my next challenge was to reach beyond behavior change and look for root causes.

CHAPTER III

The year away from home in a neighboring state passed quickly. While I was occupied with my personal problems, other events were proceeding also. My companion had finished the university work and it was soon time to think about returning home. The elements of change and movement were once more introduced into my life. How would I handle events this time? The practical aspects of packing, arranging for a mover and handling the other necessary details of moving were no problem for me. In fact I was glad to be helpful and efficient in this way. On the surface the contemplation of returning home was pleasant, even exciting. But the tentacles of Agoraphobia reach everywhere and enter into all activities. Soon I was experiencing feelings of apprehension, feelings of sadness, even the beginnings of fear. In trying to analyze these feelings, I concluded that my temporary home for a year had become, in fact, my safe place, my security. To leave meant I had to let go of this security I had built up and had come to rely on. In addition, I was leaving my therapist, my guide for so many months. I would, in a sense, be alone again. No wonder I was sad and apprehensive. There was another element to be considered in my return to my former home: facing friends and relatives again. By this time most of them had learned of my difficulties, not in any detail but at least generally. I had the feeling they would look on me differently and that prospect made me feel unsure of myself and reluctant to see people again. For some reason I was preparing myself to be on the defensive. The year away was taking on a dream-like quality. It was a paradox that I was now becoming apprehensive about returning to my own home, the place I was afraid of leaving just a short year ago. Obviously it is not just a certain place that an Agoraphobic feels comfortable, but rather it is a set of conditions which is necessary. These conditions include safety, familiarity, comfort and control. In making a home away from home I had transferred these elements from my original home to my temporary home. Since I would be leaving my temporary home, these elements would for a time exist nowhere. At least I was now able to reason through some of my feelings and understand some of the mechanisms involved. Did this fact alter my reactions or behavior? Not at all. In fact I was gradually building up a high anxiety state as our summer departure date grew nearer. I was sorry to be leaving therapy. I knew it had been only a beginning but I was grateful for what I had learned and the small progress I had made. But it was time to go.

It was early in a July morning when we made our exit. As usual I had slept little if at all the preceding night. However, I thought I had been very efficient in all the preparations that I had made ahead of time. The movers had arrived on the previous day and we had packed the car, made a lunch, gathered up our cats, left the house keys on the kitchen drain and closed the door for the last time. As we were beginning to drive away, my already dry mouth began to feel drier and I reached for the water bottle we always carried with us. It wasn't in the car. Then I realized that I had left it in the refrigerator. I knew I would never feel comfortable unless I had water readily available—and I also realized it was impossible for us to get back inside the house. After some thinking, I recalled that I had stuffed the tea kettle into the trunk of the car at the last minute. I filled it with water from the ouside faucet and we were on our way once more.

As before, it was decided that we would drive straight through without an overnight motel stop. The trip was long and tedious and I managed it fairly well until we began to see familiar landmarks. Then I was overwhelmed with mixed feelings of excitement, anticipation and sadness. The contrast between the two places and what they meant to me became very sharp. I began to experience a true nostalgia for my temporary home of a year. Perhaps because its safety for me had been so hard won, I felt close to it. Perhaps because I had experienced my first feelings of success in many years due to my therapy, I was now aware of an emptiness and a feeling of loss. My original home would be alien to me now. Others had lived in it and it was necessary for me to reclaim it.

The attachment to a safe place with familiar things is vital to the existence of an Agoraphobic. Adapting to new surroundings is at best difficult and at worst traumatic. In my case just entering my own front door was an astonishing experience. Because I had lived so recluse-like before this past year, I had a quick impression I was entering a prison. How could it be that my own home would seem hostile to me? The perversity of the idea was disturbing. Since I had been conditioned to my temporary home, my former home was a shock. I had to establish my safe place all over again. The convolutions of Agoraphobia are incredible. Because I had to be away from home for the year, I had allowed myself to completely transfer my safety needs from one place to another and now I had to find a method to reverse the process.

It took me some time to become completely at ease again with both people and places. With friends I felt the need to explain myself and my behavior. I was compelled to tell them more than they wanted to know. This was due to my feelings of uneasiness rather than their interest.

Survival places such as markets and banks presented their own problems. I used my skills of behavior modification and tried to transfer what I had previously learned.

Sometimes I was successful, sometimes I failed completely.

After I had been home for some weeks and I had made an adjustment to a routine again, I found that my anxiety and phobic reactions were recurring and with as much strength as before. The behavior modification techniques were less and less able to help me meet the demands of my life. As I noticed ordinary chores involved with shopping, visiting with friends or even entertaining at home were once more threats rather than pleasures, I wondered about the advisability of getting into therapy again.

These were very frustrating times for me because I knew I had made progress while in therapy for a year but now I experienced failure again. While entertaining at home, I often became overwhelmed with feelings of panic. I felt that I needed to flee from my own house. I couldn't pay attention to conversations and I made excuses of not being hungry when I couldn't eat with friends at my own dining room table. During these occasions I managed to get through by using alcohol as a crutch. It was the only alternative to giving in to my feelings of panic completely. When I was alone I began to examine what was happening to me since I had returned home. The obvious and honest appraisal of my condition was that I must go back into therapy. This time I knew I needed help but I was again reluctant to look for it. The thought of tracing through my long, sad history of symptoms for a new therapist seemed an impossible task. Intellectually I realized that my year of therapy had been only a beginning. I knew I had to go further but I also knew to do that would be an emotionally draining experience. In the end, my discomfort won out and I set about the task of finding a new therapist.

Choosing any professional by the random selection method can be a risky business. This is especially true when the profession concerns itself with the human condition and with individual psyches. The intensely personal nature of the one on one, therapist-patient relationship demands special characteristics to meet individual needs. I was fortunate in having an interested person refer me to a therapist of excellent reputation. But professional reputation aside, the primary consideration is always how good the rapport between the two individuals becomes. Because it is on the basis of that rapport that any progress is made for the patient, all the professional skills and good intentions in the world will not compensate for a lack of "a meeting of the minds."

One Wednesday afternoon, early in Fall, found me once again in a state of high anxiety in the office of a clinical psychologist. The strength and desperation of my feelings had given me the needed boost to seek him out and I was determined to force myself through the initial interview. It went far more easily than I had anticipated. There I was, telling my inventory of horrors to a stranger again. It is probably the desperate need to communicate that makes therapy "work" at all. Somewhere within himself the patient feels that if he can just get out enough words to interested ears, something magical will take place for him—a verbal laxative that will rid him forever of his misery. Sometimes perhaps it happens that way, but usually the words and feelings increase geometrically as the sessions go on and the process takes place. What exactly is that process and how does it take place? I am a study of only one case but I am able to describe and analyze that case with some accuracy.

The therapy process for me began very slowly. I was in need again of establishing for myself a safe place, a safe person, an anchor for myself. I also felt an unmet need to bring my intellect to bear on my condition. I was not too keen on increasing my repertoire of desensitization techniques as I felt I had learned them well during the previous year. Therefore, during my initial sessions with my new therapist, we took the time to go over my life chronologically and to also go into the history of the development of my symptoms of Agoraphobia. Obviously there had to be causes, some of which became clear after a time, and others which are obscure and will probably always remain so. We had weekly sessions—every Wednesday afternoon—and I was soon learning much about myself and about my illness.

It is obvious that part of the process in therapy takes place between the therapist and the patient. The components of this part of the therapy are questions, answers, speculations, tears, half thoughts, and sometimes poorly formed ideas. There is a mutual attempt to try to put some sense and direction into a muddled life situation. The other part of the process is slower, less logical, and private. This part belongs to the patient alone. It consists of sudden insights, or insights which are not sudden and represent a long gestation period. In addition to insight, a re-evaluation take place. Old priorities give way, familiar rationalizations may seem ill-conceived and outdated. When conditions are optimal, the patient is aware of these changes and can see progress and has a reason to hope. There is nothing automatic in this process. In fact, it requires a great amount of work. Many times there is resistance to a change in thinking, resistance to an emotional change, or resistance to an idea. The patient then does battle with himself in an attempt to reject the old approaches and accept the new. Not only is intellectual conviction important in this process, but emotional commitment is equally important. In its barest essentials, therapy is a process of filtering the life experiences of one individual through the medium of another individual, and then examining those experiences again from a shared perspective. It is out of this new perspective that emotional health and sometimes life itself is restored. If it is an ego trip, perhaps it should be. After all, it is the sick and shattered ego that leads to the therapist in the first place.

As I said, for me therapy was a slow process. I was still unconvinced that a probing of my development would lead to an elimination of my Agoraphobia. At the same time, I knew that the simple, direct method I had followed for a year was not the complete answer either. If I wanted to be rid of my horrors, I had to proceed in a new direction. I had to find out three things: why I had the depression; why I had the fear; and could I function normally again?

48

For me at this stage it was important to provide answers as well as techniques which changed my behavior.

In the beginning of our Wednesday session, we, in effect, set aside the Agoraphobia and changed the focus to my life history and the dynamics of my development to that point. Here I was female, forty-eight, single, bright; a lifetime summation in four words. What went wrong?

Taken in the order of their listing, the first thing to go wrong was that I was born female. It may not still be a man's world, but forty-eight years ago it was very much a man's world. Females were the original second-class citizens. It was not that there was open hostility toward girl children, it was just that the limits on behavior were so circumscribed and the idealization of the female role was so institutionalized, that any evidence of departure from this norm was prohibited. I departed from the norm from the beginning. As a young female I was not conscious of how inappropriate my interests were. I wasn't exactly a tomboy, but I was far from the stereotype little girl. As I reached school age, it was obvious that I was bright. Bright children can be a threat to the adults around them. Especially for females, brightness at that time was not acceptable. The standard was for girls to be pretty, nurturing, manipulative, but not too bright. Although I grew up under this standard, I was in constant conflict with it. My earliest self concept did not allow me to picture myself in the roles that biology had supposedly prescribed for me. Without knowing why, I rebelled inwardly whenever I was told that I could not do something because I was a girl. I felt great confidence in myself and my abilities and could see no reason why I couldn't do and be whatever I wanted. However, for the most part, I performed outwardly in the expected the conventional way. I was polite, obedient, and tried to do things to please the adults around me. There was one area, however, where I would not allow myself to conform. I had a true interest in the life of the mind, in ideas. I was fond of books, of science, and interested in all the questions concerning human behavior. I would approach members of my family with questions which were usually in an area of interest outside their ability to answer. Sometimes I was made to understand that my interests and questions were inappropriate for a girl. Mysteriously, certain areas of knowledge and information were reserved for males. When I asked why this was so, I was told that's how things are. In time I learned to keep my questioning mind to myself while at the same time I was learning what would please the adults around me. The existence of this situation was the reason for my developing a secret life. It was necessary for me to have some means of self-expression, some way that I could allow the real me to emerge. My secret life was not one of subterfuge, since no one had any knowledge of its existence. Nor was it the usual fantasy world that children often make for themselves. It was more that I realized at an early age that, in a sense, I spoke a different language from that of my family. I had different concerns and, in fact, I was developing a different set of values. My reading, the kind of associates I had, these things became very private matters. On the surface I behaved in a conforming way and only occasionally did I allow the real, different me to show through to my family. One of these occasions was to be a sore point for the rest of my life. I expressed the desire to study medicine and to become a surgeon. I was reminded by my family members that since I was a girl, my role was to marry and have children like all the other girls. I would have a husband who would take care of me so I wouldn't have to become a surgeon Besides very few girls went to medical school. Encounters such as this and variations of the theme continued over the years of childhood and into adolescence and had a searing effect on my development. It seemed so strange that the people who presumably loved me, did not understand me—or did not want to.

In one of the paradoxes life offers us, I somehow developed a strength and belief in myself that became part of my personal equipment until the onset of the symptoms of Agoraphobia. When I entered high school, I found I had no problem with anything in the academic area and so I took college prep courses. By this time, having become well aware of the world of the mind, I discovered that I was not alone in my interests anymore. I still met with family resistance but now I had other recourses for my intellectual companionship. But I was still hurt that not a single family member really knew or understood me. So I turned outward for the appreciation I needed.

I was growing and developing in two distinctly different directions. The nominal me was part of a conventional family. I appeared to be simply another member of a later generation. The other me was a social, intellectual, and political rebel. What was I rebelling from? It was obvious that the conventional and limiting family I was surrounded by offered no understanding of my developing needs. There were countless times when I wanted to share my feelings or a special interest I had developed in some aspect of my education. When I made an overture toward my family, I was rebuffed directly or ridiculed for my ideas. Because I was allowed no overt way to express my individuality, I found my outlet in being a rebel intellectually. I formed ideas and opinions which were not conventional. My friends were chosen for their differences, for what I saw as rebellion in them. I cultivated my interest in the arts and literature independently. I sought out ideas and concepts that were not in the main stream of thought. I was, in short, a rebel underneath my skin and a conformist on the outside. As the years went by, I became more and more disillusioned and saddened at having to play these two roles. Time after time, in some attempt to establish communication, I would approach a family member and try to elicit interest in my concerns. And time after time, I was rebuffed. It took a long time to learn that things would never be different. Perhaps I never did learn it completely.

How did this experience when growing up bear on the development of Agoraphobia? Because Agoraphobia appears, at this time, to afflict more women than men, it may be appropriate to question whether the traditional role descriptions for women which are passed from generation to generation may not be a factor in the onset of problems such as Agoraphobia. That all women are not afflicted with the problem simply means that all women are not dissatisfied with the conventional female role. For those who are and who find all avenues blocked for the expression of their feelings, for those who find that the roles society and custom have prescribed for females are limited and confining and frustrating, it is little wonder that the bizarre symptoms characteristic of Agoraphobia could develop. If a life situation or role is in basic conflict with some part of the personality, eventually some symptoms of that conflict will become manifest. It is not possible to indefinitely suppress an important part of the psyche without neurotic symptoms developing. The precise time at which symptoms will become obvious will vary with the life circumstances of each individual, and may depend on some crisis or difficult life situation. The neurosis of choice for many women with role conflicts such as my own appears to be Agoraphobia. I do not mean that the symptoms are deliberately chosen, but rather that they appear as a response to the conflicts over a mixed identity. Functionally, through the Agoraphobia, a woman is rejecting all the aspects of an assigned role which was not freely chosen by her. The way in which she shows the rejection behaviorally is in the form of withdrawal from active participation in life, as well as an unreasonable and uncontrollable fear of everything. Eventually the condition become totally incapacitating. Developing with the other behavioral changes is a depression which is probably partly a product of the frustration of dealing with the Agoraphobia itself, and partly a basic cause of the symptoms in the first place. Given the fact that individual cases will vary in specific symptoms or in personal details, it is more or less likely that Agoraphobia is present in females more than in males because females are confronted from the beginning with the possibility of a role conflict in their lives if they are not naturally accepting of the traditional roles they have historically been assigned. One does not have to be an ardent feminist to be aware of the inequities which have been a part of women's lives since time began. Even if rebellion against these inequities is not on a conscious level, it can make its presence known by the development of a neurosis such as Agoraphobia.

In my personal case, the dichotomy between what I believed was expected of me and what I wanted for myself became greater as time went by, and as many aspects of my life grew unsatisfactory to me. When you are not wholly accepted as you are, but are constantly subjected to hurtful criticism or ridicule, a strange thing can happen: in an effort to gain approval from others and to gain acceptance by them, one can try very hard to acquire those characteristics others demand. But in doing this, a schism is created in the personality, since part of the individual is what he feels himself to be, on his own terms. In my life, this schism developed and grew to the point where I gradually developed the symptoms of Agoraphobia. I found in my first year of therapy that the application of palliative treatment for my symptoms did nothing to help my understanding of how to deal with this schism in myself. At the beginning of my second year, I was to see how the pieces fit together and how I could use that understanding to help myself.

For many Agoraphobics, the greatest help they can imagine is something, anything, which will restore them to normal feelings and behavior. To be able to function in the real world would be considered "cure" enough. In many cases this can be achieved with exposure techniques and behavior modification. Having experienced a year of this approach, my symptoms were lessened, I could function more appropriately, but I really understood little of the real nature of my illness. I felt a need to know as much as possible about Agoraphobia and how it became a part of my life. Intensive, personal therapy was the only way to look for these answers. I took on this challenge with the results to be detailed further along in this writing.

Second in the concise description of myself: female, forty-eight, single, bright; is my age at the time I entered into therapy.

When a woman reaches her middle years and shows any symptoms or psychological and/or physical discomfort concomitant with advancing maturity, it is assumed that the first condition (discomfort) is caused by the second condition (age). Medical doctors, particularly, seem to have a predeliction for placing every illness into the category of "just part of the menopause." Unfortunately, there are just enough instances of where the symptoms are indicative of having been caused by the condition of menopause to keep the myth alive. But as every woman knows, or will come to know, there are other changes which are coincident with the last half of life which have nothing to do with menopause. These changes offer a diagnostic challenge to any doctor, if he is interested, and may prove to be a dilemma for the woman, if he is not interested.

Like everyone, I became age-aware in my forties. I was not afflicted with feelings of impending death, but I was suddenly acutely aware of the passage of time. Somehow all the great plans which I had for myself were getting farther away from attainment. I felt myself caught in the "it's now or never" bind. It was also at this age that I began to notice the first overt symptoms of Agoraphobia. Of course, I had no idea what was happening to me psychologically, since I was interpreting my symptoms as having physical causes. When I noticed excessive fatigue, and my lack of interest in socializing, or the strange attacks of anxiety now and then, I attributed it to too many long hours in my real estate work. Later as the symptoms became more frequent and persistent and as they began to interfere with my work, I decided it was time to see my physician. He suggested that menopause was the primary cause of my problems and prescribed a tranquilizer. Not satisfied with this diagnosis, I consulted another doctor. His conclusions were that I had either the early symptoms of Multiple Sclerosis or that my physical problems were psychological (translate: menopause).

It must be noted in fairness that the symptoms of Agoraphobia are confusing and could be mistaken for a variety of physical illnesses. While psychologists and psychiatrists may be faulted for diagnosing Agoraphobia as anxiety neurosis, general physicians must be forgiven if they are unable to separate the symptoms of this problem. However, they cannot be forgiven for placing all the problems of mature women under the rubric of menopause.

As I noted earlier in this writing, I was reluctant to see my problems in psychological terms. I was equally reluctant to see my problems as the product of my becoming older. This difficulty, this lack of real communication between others and myself added to my growing feelings of frustration about finding out the source of my symptoms. Not only did I have to survive the fact of being female but also now I had to accommodate the additional jeopardy of being or becoming middle aged.

The middle years can be thought of as a challenge to the re-creative aspects of a person's life. It can be a time for second careers, second loves, even a complete new lifestyle. However, it is sometimes none of these things, but becomes instead a time for recriminations and regrets. Awareness of individual mortality is then acute, as the passage of time means going down the hill rather than climbing up it. All of these realizations can be damaging to the self-concept. In my case, I was more and more aware of the fact that I had never done many of the things I had told myself I could, would do. There was no way that I could fight the passage of time. My lack of accomplishment seemed a huge question that I could find no explanation for. Surely by now I had stopped caring what my family thought of my accomplishments or the lack of them. In fact, I had been estranged from my family for some time. But I was still haunted by my years of childhood and adolescence when I was often criticized for being myself. I was often told that there was really only one of two choices for me to make, that I had two alternatives in life: marry well and this meant success; or try to make it on your own, and this meant failure. My self-concept now had to face the fact that here I was with half a lifetime gone and perhaps well on my way to fulfilling the second part of the prophecy that I would fail. Being told by doctors that my physical problems were due to aging somehow translated for me that my body was also a failure and that there was nothing I could do about it but live it out. I responded to this situation by developing a deep depression. I was depressed about my past and I was also depressed about my future. Now as the insidious symptoms of Agoraphobia began to appear in earnest, they joined my state of depression. A cycle of depression combined with fears, producing more depression began, and I was unable to find any way to stop the interaction of these two elements in my life. Depression is most likely to be present with Agoraphobia, to some degree at least. It would be most unusual for a person to be faced on a moment to moment basis with the miserable symptoms of Agoraphobia and not become generally depressed. Added to this is the almost total lack of understanding of the disorder by professionals, let alone treatment for it, and it is little wonder that depression becomes a factor in the illness. The tranquilizers which were prescribed for me by my physician actually aggravated the depression I had developed and, as mentioned earlier, the tranquilizers had little or no effect in reducing the anxiety and panic attacks of Agoraphobia itself. It seemed to me that besides my lifelong dismay at being female, I now had the additional burden of my age to cope with.

Growing older is certainly a fact of life, but for some reason, it is the female who is constantly reminded that her problems are a result of this process. This is especially true when she is treated by male doctors. It is interesting to note in passing that male Agoraphobics do not report having been told by their doctors that their symptoms were due to the onset of middle age.

Fortunately for me, with some creative probing during my second year of therapy, I was able to sort out those conditions which were due to my age, and those conditions which were part of my neurosis. But the memory of having been given a medical and intellectual "brush-off" by those professionals who prefer to deal with people in terms of generalities rather than take the time to see each patient as an individual, will always be strong and clear. How many incorrect diagnoses have been hidden under the umbrella of menopause and tranquilizers may never be known. There is no doubt that there is a mid-life crisis for most people and it takes varied forms and can be of long or short duration. The significant aspects of my personal mid-life crisis revolved around the development of Agoraphobia and its depression and not the fact that I was progressing from one decade to another.

My next defining characteristic is that I am, and always have been, single. I suppose that this fact is the result of both choice and circumstance. It is the result of choice because it is the one thing over which I have never allowed any external control. It has been my personal decision at all times. Circumstance has also conspired to allow for my single state. Since I have always desired a career for myself rather than seeing myself in a conventional role as wife and mother, I was careful to avoid circumstances which could interfere with that goal. So, as I grew up through my adolescence and into young womanhood, I made a conscious decision to remain unmarried. This was often a difficult decision to defend and I had to defend it often. The day of the "swinging single" was far in the future, and any young woman who did not marry by a reasonable age was suspect, or, at the very least, open to jokes about old maids.

Being single also had its less amusing aspects. The universal complaint of women that, married or single, they often had to endure the unwanted attention of male bosses or fellow workers, was familiar to me. Many times, because I was single, it was assumed that I was also available and interested. Often a polite rebuff was not sufficiently discouraging and it was necessary to become more assertive concerning my feelings. It is demeaning to have to try to maintain your personal integrity as a female and at the same time spare the feelings of the male who just insulted you. Being single was a mixed bag for me. While it afforded me the kind of freedom I wanted and left my options open, it also presented me with the problem of either constant explanations or constant rebuffing.

It has been observed that there are certain characteristics or personality traits which Agoraphobics have in common. Among these traits is a strong desire to please, to be polite, not to offend. This particularly characteristic is a problem for Agoraphobics (especially women), as they go out of their way not to offend the person who is offending them. This type of caution tends to reinforce the fear and withdrawing behavior which is part of Agoraphobia. Paradoxically, an Agoraphobic may become angry and hostile toward the offender but will repress this legitimate anger and, therefore, become withdrawn and non-assertive. This latter description was true in my case. The continual questioning and joking about myself often made me very angry. It angered me because I interpreted the comments about myself as a "single career woman" as an implied insult to my intelligence and to my person. To me the implication was that somehow a single woman did not have the capacity or strengths to make a life for herself without the cushion of marriage. In addition, my career choices in the male-dominated medical and psychological fields were bad choices if I wanted to avoid criticism. In the considered view of both family and friends, I would be much better off and much happier if I would give up my single nonsense, get married and settle down.

This aspect of my personal history has bearing on the development of Agoraphobia generally, because it is an example of one more way in which a woman can be harassed to the point where it becomes a question of pleasing others or pleasing oneself. In psychological terms, ego strength is severely tested against the strength of family and peer pressure. In many cases, with a strong and healthy ego, this whole thing is a trivial problem. But for the Agoraphobic, anything which attacks the ego further erodes the self-confidence. The thought that what one is thinking or doing or being is looked upon as foolish or wrong is the worst sort of criticism, since it attacks the essential nature of an individual. Agoraphobics do not respond well to criticism, especially personal criticism. Since the self-image of the Agoraphobic is poor, criticism only serves to aggravate the negative feelings of self-worth. As I progressed through the various stages of therapy, I found that one of the most difficult tasks my therapist and I shared was that of restoring my self-image to a healthy state. Because I had spent such a great amount of energy in constantly defending myself and my preferences against the opinions of others, by the time I was Agoraphobic and in therapy, my ego strength and self-esteem were at its lowest point. I had not fully realized how dismal I felt about myself and my life prospects until I began to build up a feeling of confidence again with the help of my therapist. A flattened ego is difficult to pump up. It has arrived at its battered state by degrees over time and it is very hard to undo the harmful effects. It is often difficult to see the relationship between current behavior and past causes of the behavior. One of the aspects of therapy which is vital to its success is the ability to understand the connection between these two points. It appears that it is possible for the human psyche to store uncomfortable messages and experiences and to show a reaction to them at some later time. This later appearance of a delayed response is often seen in the development of a neurosis. When the response develops at a later time, it is then misplaced and inappropriate and becomes part of the neurotic symptoms such as I exhibited in Agoraphobia.

Current research into the personality development of Agoraphobics and the comparison of childhood memories by those in therapy or in self-help groups, indicates that the development of Agoraphobic characteristics and symptoms appears in early childhood. Therefore, childhood experiences are crucial in terms of whether they augment the other factors which may contribute to the development of Agoraphobia. A sensitive, compliant, intelligent child whose parents and others are overly critical and demanding may be laying the groundwork for the child's neurosis of the future.

In the long course of my therapy, my therapist and I began to put together the relationships between past causes and my current behavior. The relationship seems clear enough: after spending my childhood and adolescence trying to please others, trying to fit in, looking for love and understanding, while at the same time trying to deal with my own notions of self, which were often in conflict with how I was perceived by others, my reserve of psychological strength and feelings of self-worth were exhausted. It was in response to this loss of self that the symptoms of Agoraphobia and depression developed. Because I was no longer able to find a middle ground of thinking and doing that would please everyone, including myself, I opted out of life. It took the form of Agoraphobia, but what was really happening was that I was through with defending and apologizing for my sex, my age, my marital status and the quantity and quality of my intelligence. Psychologically it was a question of retaining my personal integrity even if I became emotionally ill to do it.

The final element in my succinct self-description category was "bright." I placed this characteristic in last position because, of all of them, being bright has caused me the greatest difficulty. In a sense, my own intelligence has contributed to my image problems, and, therefore, to my developing Agoraphobia.

There was no doubt from earliest childhood that I was a brighter than average child. At first this fact seemed to please my family. My mother, particularly, took great delight in showing me off to friends and strangers alike. I learned to read before I attended school and I could recite many poems from memory at a very early age. I also showed great curiosity and when I was young this was considered "cute." However, as time passed and I grew older, members of my family were often put off by my endless questions and by the scope of my interests. As I mentioned earlier, a too bright child can be threatening to a parent. To most of my questions I was given an answer that was meant to put me off until some later time (which never arrived). I found this not only frustrating but I became more and more reluctant to pose questions at home, consequently, I sought other sources of information. My family did not realize that for me, answers were not only necessary, they were also essential for my development. I do not want to imply that I was a genius child nor was I especially talented in any one area. I was a quick and clever child, more able to analyze and synthesize information than was the average child. I developed an early liking for language, for words. I had an almost intuitive understanding of relationships, both technical and non-technical. I was able, at a very early age, to conceptualize and to use the principles of logic in my thinking and when presenting my ideas. This type of verbal precocity offered mild amusement to some members of my family and, as I have said, was a threat to others. It was a threat I suspect because they did not know whether to accept me as a challenge or to reject me as a misfit, a strange child. It was the ambiguity of the situation which troubled them most. When some notion that I had was shown to be foolish or some plan would eventuate in failure, members of my family were quick to point out to me that I was not so "smart" after all. Paradoxically, I was sometimes challenged by my family to come up with the solution to a problem, to find an answer, since I was "so smart." These alternating attitudes toward me in this area were hard to contend with as a child and also as a young adult. As time went on, I concluded that the predominant family feeling toward me was one of

61

dismay.

Boys do not like girls who are too smart. So I was often cautioned to let boys take the lead in conversations, and certainly in decision making. This made one more demand on me to appear different from the way I was. Another charade in the name of conforming and pleasing others and I went along with it for some time. I was fortunate in my adolescence to have friends who were also bright and whose families applauded and encouraged their brightness. It was a sharp contrast, observing the attitude of my friends' parents compared to the attitude of my own family. I envied them, but at least I was comforted by the knowledge that I was not some strange creature who did not fit into the scheme of things.

Damage to the ego is seldom the result of one encounter in life. It is more often an accumulation of small hurts presented to the self from time to time. Worst of all, the hurts seem to validate a feeling of being unsure of one's true worth. After a time, real doubt sets in, as it did for me in my family setting. As I began to encounter the larger world outside my family, I found that I was not that odd in my brightness, in my need to know and to understand the world inside me and around me.

It was out of the associations with my friends and their families that I gained a lifelong respect for the finer turnings of the human mind. Had I not had this outlet, I might have allowed myself to eventually conform in full to what my own family expected of me. And so it happened that as with other characteristics of my personality, my behavior and thinking were also dichotomized in the intellectual areas. When I was in the company of my family, I would leave the world of ideas and concern myself with their interests. The result of this type of behavior was that I had no sense of discipline where intellectual pursuits were concerned. Since I always had intense interests, and I certainly had the potential, I must feel that, had I received more encouragement, I would have found the discipline to develop those interests more seriously and earlier than I did.

In my young adult life, my brightness had an effect on my job prospects. I learned by trial and error not to appear too bright on tests and interviews which I took for positions. Any above average understanding of what was required for the job was a guarantee of being called over-qualified. Interviewers sometimes said that they were sure I would soon become bored with the job and, therefore, would not stay on the job. It was reason enough not to hire me in their minds. Any protest from me that I needed the money fell on deaf ears. It was also often assumed by prospective employers that I was planning to go on to higher education and that any career that did not include higher education requirements was a waste of my time. It was strange to realize that in the work world I was not wanted because of my intelligence. Of course, this was not the case in all instances and I did have jobs where my talents were used and, in some cases, challenged. I may have chosen to go into real estate so that I could be free of the necessity of working for someone other than myself.

In contemporary society, it is now more acceptable for a woman to be both "brainy" and employable. However, I still have moments when I encounter one of two responses to my intelligence. I hear, "you are so bright, it seems such a waste. . . ." or "if you're so smart, why aren't you president?, rich?, etc." Comments such as these are more embarrassing than amusing. To have an interest and not to have this interest produce a career or a financial reward is to be in an unpopular position. Society seems to view a well developed intelligence as an available, communal resource rather than as an individual's private possession.

Socially, at least in some circles, my brightness as shown by my conversational interests, has sometimes been a handicap. Most social gatherings prefer the light touch, while my preference has been to share ideas.

After adolescence, I did not play the game of bright boy and dull girl any longer. As a consequence of this decision, I have met interesting and challenging minds of both sexes now and then. But in the general run of things, pedestrian ideas and conversations dominate most of living and serve to remind me of how difficult it has been to adjust to this fact.

It is probable that Agoraphobics will be found on the higher side of the IQ curve. The dynamics of the neurosis could be considered sophisticated. The fact that Agoraphobics withdraw from active participation in life could indicate an over-sensitive awareness of all the hypocrisy, duplicity, and general difficulty there is in living. This acute awareness causes the intellect to be brought to bear on the status quo, and finding it wanting, rejects it. Speculation aside, my personal experience has made me dubious about the value of a large supply of intelligence. When I was so reluctant to acknowledge that I was having personal psychological problems, it was partly due to my belief that I could intellectualize my own problems, bring my intelligence to bear on things and change them. Obviously this approach was not successful and I can see in retrospect that it was my own intelligence that almost kept me from helping myself. Recalling my childhood, it was expected that I would bring home good grades from school. When I sought some reward for this behavior, I was told that since I was always expected to do well, there was nothing to reward. I was simply living up to everyone's expectations. Later I became ambivalent concerning my own intellectual gifts. Success as its own reward came to mean less and less to me and I found myself in the position of failure without realizing that I had put myself there because of my own indifference.

There is an additional element that has made being bright of less value to me: that is having to find excuses, to have to apologize for not using my mind in some more productive way. Often after some few minutes of conversation, a new acquaintance has found reason to ask what I did. When told, the reaction was disappointment that I did not have a higher status, a more important job title.

While the state of my ego was being enhanced on the one hand, I was tearing it down by my efforts at explaining and apologizing for myself. The end result of all this was that a supposed asset became, instead, a liability.

Within the process of therapy it is necessary to bring the intelligence to bear on what the emotions try to convey and a well functioning brain can be of great help. But in the end, no amount of intellect prevented me from developing an emotional illness which caused me to waste many years of my life.

The concise description of myself under the four headings of female, forty-eight, single, bright, present a framework on which to place my individual life. But more importantly, an analysis of each of the four dimensions suggests how they may have interacted and to what extent that interaction may have contributed to the development of my Agoraphobia. It is possible to hypothesize that when the development of the essential nature of a person is interfered with from childhood, causing a development which suits other's expectations rather than the individual's own expectations, there will come a time when the internal conflict which results will become manifest as some type of mental or emotional illness. Further, when the person affected is female, it is likely she will develop Agoraphobia. Age of onset, symptoms, idiosyncratic fears and anxieties will vary with the individual but the basic avoidance behavior characteristic of Agoraphobia will always be present.

Looking analytically at my own case, it is possible to trace the dynamics of my ego destruction and the consequent development of my overwhelming fears. As a child it was obvious that I was not pleasing to my immediate family. When I tried to please both myself and my family, a schism developed around whose expectations were to be met — mine or others. When we are young and the ego is constantly adjusting and appraising, it is possible to live with paradox and ambiguity. Or at least to appear to live with it more successfully than when we are older. Maturity brings with it either compromise or a more difficult task of dealing with others and with self simultaneously. When the ego development is stifled or diverted to directions which are not comfortable or natural for the individual, it is to be expected that a struggle will result as the essential nature of an individual tries to protect its own integrity. The neurotic behavior which results in a human adaptation, an attempt to control. Control is a dominant and important factor in the life of an Agoraphobic. Because he has abdicated all control of his life to others expectations, he is left with only one option. . .and that is withdrawal. This action of withdrawal involves a complex dynamic in which the much desired control factor is present in the breech. Although in the case of Agoraphobia, it seems that there is an abandoning of any attempt to control behavior on the part of the victim; in fact, what happens is exactly the opposite. His own survival demands that an Agoraphobic control those people, places and things in his environment that give rise to his anxieties and fears. As the neurosis develops and becomes the dominant thing in his life, he finally exercises the ultimate control. He removes himself from all disturbing stimuli. He cuts himself off from all external life around him as he tries to deal with his own feelings. If he receives help from therapy and insight develops, it becomes possible to deal with not only the symptoms of Agoraphobia but also to deal with the underlying causes. The syndrome that is called Agoraphobia is merely the surface, symptomatic, indication of the underlying problem which is a sick and battered ego. The symptoms of Agoraphobia, then, are the last-ditch effort of an individual to cope with his life situation. At last he has lost the ability to pretend or to please others or to offer excuses for his behavior or his feelings. Short of self-destruction, his alternative is to resort to a greater and greater withdrawal from life. Psychologically he is withdrawing from the role he has played for the benefit of others and by avoiding active participation in living, he can also avoid directly hurting those whose plans for him he wants

66

to reject. Instead of rejecting them obviously, he covers his act of rejection by making it a general act of non-participation. In this way, no "other" is offended and the Agoraphobic can try to save what's left of himself for himself. On the surface this behavior places no blame except on the individual himself. To the observer, it appears obvious that the Agoraphobic is causing, or at least aiding, in the production of his own fear behavior. This is an entirely appropriate characterization since, as noted earlier, one of the personality traits which Agoraphobics have in common is the desire to please others; to never offend. The common dread of being overwhelmed by fear in front of others and thus embarrassing them is a part of the loss of ego strength and poor feelings of self-worth which characterize the problem. Everything can be a threat to a deteriorating ego and the more the Agoraphobic moves away from life, the better he controls the threats. His behavior does not help his sick ego but it does help to keep the displaced anxiety and fear responses at bay. By not attending the theater or not entering the market to shop, the Agoraphobic does not have to experience the bizarre symptoms he hates to deal with. Each time he avoids those things which are problem areas for him, he reinforces that avoiding behavior so that in time the boundaries of comfortable living become extremely narrow.

In my individual case, the part of myself that had always tried to develop and be accepted was so diverted from emergence by strong parental and family influences that its survival was only possible by the development of an illness. This was not a conscious choice and in fact it took years before I was aware of it at all. By becoming so psychologically ill that I was forced to seek professional help, that part of me which had been mostly hidden all my life was going to have an outlet at last. Had I not been repressed and ridiculed in my developing years, but instead had been praised and encouraged in my uniqueness, it is doubtful that I would have ever developed Agoraphobia. But had I never developed Agoraphobia, I would not have taken part in the therapy process which has led me to some understanding of my own case and of the dynamics of human behavior in general.

CHAPTER IV

Psychotherapy or therapy is a process by which change in thinking and behavior takes place. It is not something that is done *to* you, nor is it a process in which the patient is merely a passive participant. On the contrary, to be effective, the therapy process has to be entered into actively by both therapist and patient. Something must transpire between the two participants in order for anything to change for the illness. The "talking cure" has validity today much as it did when Freud first named it. Critics have said that the patient leaves therapy having done nothing more that substitute one rationale for another. If that is the least of it and the rationale derived from the therapy process makes for a healthier psyche, then what has been lost — only the illness. But the therapy process is more than just word games between therapist and patient. Because it is a process, it is made up of discrete bits of change which together form a mosaic on which a cure can be fashioned. Often the bits of change take place without the immediate conscious awareness of the patient. On the other hand, often there is conscious resistance to change. Letting go of bad habits or non-productive thought patterns is very difficult to do, especially for the neurotic. As time goes by, the therapy process functions in spite of the resistance of the patient and little by little, subtle changes begin to take place. Lifelong patterns of emotional reaction are examined by the therapist and the patient together. Even habits of thought and types of motivation are placed under careful scrutiny. What comes out of this examination of self with the help of another is a re-evaluation, a change of perspective that can help to give new priorities to the people and events that have shaped the patient's life and may have contributed to his illness. Bringing a new or different perspective to bear on things is not the same as dismissing them as unimportant or disguising them so that they are unrecognizable. In fact, part of the therapy process is to help the patient to confront and deal with those things which have not been faced in the past, or which have been faced in a way that has contributed to poor emotional or mental health. When past behavior is dealt with under the discipline of current therapy, new insights and understandings can take place which help to assuage the hurt and anger and disappointment that has resulted in unhappy, neurotic behavior.

I have mentioned that during the therapy process the patient is an active participant. This active participation means that many times the patient deliberately brings into focus those things that are present in his life which are painful for him to deal with. It is a continuous surprise how much material comes to the surface during therapy sessions. On many occasions I have contemplated a therapy appointment, wondering what I could possibly have to discuss, let alone reveal. During the session, I am amazed at what transpires and how much material I have dealt with. If there is a magic involved in the process, it possibly is present during the self-revealing moments that are unexpected. Skeletons appear which test the courage to face them. Events, feelings, memories, which were assumed to be long buried, rise to the surface. Within the therapy process they must be dealt with openly and thoroughly. All of this requires active participation on the part of the patient. Going through this process is like an emotional and intellectual purgative. It is not a pleasant ego trip. It requires courage, dedication and conviction that something takes place besides the passage of time.

For me the most difficult aspect of the therapy process was learning to admit that I was sick and understanding that there were reasons for my illness. On the surface it would appear that the fact of seeking professional help implied acceptance of the presence of illness. Unfortunately it is not that simple. I found that even while I was a patient, there were times in the beginning of therapy when I felt I could handle my own problems and administer my own cures. This attitude did not stem from pure ego, but rather a belief in my own knowledge. I had come to believe in myself intellectually and to feel that I could handle any intellectual challenge. What I did not perceive about myself was that I was emotionally ill and that my background and understanding could not possibly help me deal with my sick feelings. The situation required an objective evaluation and help and I was to receive just that as time went by. It was a combination of feelings that I dealt with at first. I was embarrassed and reluctant to talk about my sessions. I was sure all of my friends would see me differently from now on. I hated the fact that someone was delving into my past and that I was actually paying to have it happen. After my beginning therapy sessions, I was very fatigued and angry at myself for going through such a process. There were countless nights when my sleep was disturbed by dreams out of a past which I thought was long forgotten. I also held theoretical discussions and sometimes arguments with my therapist; all in my head. My whole life seemed to revolve around my therapy sessions in the same way it had revolved around my Agoraphobia prior to therapy. Many times when I was caught up in the activity of my own talking during a session, I would later wonder why I had responded in a certain way or why certain material was selected by my brain for emphasis. In most of my sessions, other than answering informational questions, I was free to approach any aspect of my feelings, memories, experiences that I wanted to bring up.

In the course of these dialogues, every now and then a glimmer of light would appear, a small connection would be made. At these times, I could know that I had insight into the puzzle of my own life. There were other times when it was not until after the session that the best and clearest connections would be made. These were connections made between my symptoms of Agoraphobia and the events of my life which caused them to develop. As always the most valuable understanding is the kind that is gained through personal effort. My understanding of the near destruction of my ego was gradually gained in this manner. With the care and guidance of my therapist, I finally learned to face up to the fact that the schism in my personality which grew up with me caused me to become not two persons, but no person. Unconsciously, I had become aware of this event and had developed the symptoms of Agoraphobia as a way of handling my unsolved problems.

In one sense, I had to reject the world around me and everything in it in order to save myself. Because I had grown up unsure of my own self-worth, I had assumed the role that would please those around me. I made too many adjustments and compromises and as my life reached its middle years, I developed my emotional illness. In the course of my therapy, I realized how the groundwork for this illness had been laid by myself and by others during my childhood and adolescence. I had to face the fact that I, too, had contributed to my illness. I allowed myself to believe in the value systems and judgments of my relatives. They told me I could never be a success in my field of interest and I believed them. I did not consciously agree with their evaluation of me, but unconsciously, I allowed their judgments to become my judgments. I bought the script they had designed for me as surely as if I had written it myself. After this type of self-knowledge is revealed through therapy, it is natural to wonder why it was not known before without all the suffering that led up to the knowledge. Unfortunately, our emotional and psychological systems are not simple. The self-delusion and the subterfuge that we permit ourselves throughout our lives keep real knowledge of ourselves from ourselves. The shock of coming face to face with a sick and negative side of our personal development is not easy to absorb. It may be for this reason that psychotherapy seems to be such a slow process. If it were quick it is doubtful that much self-understanding could take place, let alone believed. It is in this connection that a good therapist is most appreciated. By guiding the patient as he comes to understand his illness, and by helping to make some sense out of the paradoxes and illogic of his experiences, a good therapist can make the difference between frightening illness and comfortable health.

When the truth about the reasons for my developing Agoraphobia began to emerge, I, at first, was skeptical. I could not see the relationship between my sick ego as the result of my family's lack of interest and understanding, and my symptoms which kept me from now leading a normal life. As the pieces began to fall into place, my next reaction was resistance, even hostility to the idea that I could be so manipulated by others, even if it had happened unconsciously. I had spent a good part of my life studying human behavior and I thought I understood my own. Seeing at last that I could fall prey to the maneuvering and manipulations of others was a further blow to my ego. I wondered where my intelligence had gone. How could I permit myself to become sick because of something that had happened so long ago? But more importantly, what could I do now that I did understand the problem to prevent the rest of my life from being wasted also?

I have said that therapy often leads to insights. However, insights are not answers. It does not automatically follow that because we can gain an intellectual understanding of something, we can, therefore, gain emotional control of it, too. In the original process of conditioning that takes place when we learn something, there is often an emotional response that accompanies the learning. The emotional response may sometimes be inappropriate or even pathological, but because it is a concomitant of the learning itself, it is retained along with whatever intellectual process has taken place. Just as it is often difficult to learn new facts to take the place of old ones, it is very difficult to learn a new or more appropriate emotional response which can take the place of the old one. This point became clear to me as I tried to apply my understandings of my symptoms of Agoraphobia to the day to day situations I was confronted with. My intellect was fully aware of the fact that because my self-confidence was gone, I had trouble making decisions in supermarkets or sometimes even entering stores and shops. This knowledge gave me an understanding of *what* the problem was but I needed more to learn *how* to overcome it. It was in this respect that the techniques used in behavior modification therapy came to my aid. With these techniques I could deliberately set a goal for myself; for example, fifteen minutes in the supermarket. Since I knew I was free to leave at the end of fifteen minutes, I was able to manage the short amount of time without panic. The next time out I would increase the allotted time or go to a different store which might be further from my home. The important thing was to have a specific goal and that I should set it for myself. In this way I was not only reconditioning myself as far as my response to a previously feared situation but I was also gaining control over my own life again. I was not always successful in the application of these principles and when the anxiety in a situation became too great for me to handle, I withdrew from the situation. It was during times of failure that I had to remind myself that my worth as a person was not diminished and that it was alright to try again. Learning that failure does not diminish the personal worth is one of the most difficult lessons of therapy. We are so convinced from childhood that what we do is what we are that failure means failure of the self. When ego structure is damaged or destroyed, until it is re-built, any failure assumes proportions out of context. My mind found it easy to process this information but my emotions resisted it all the way. I was terrified of failure but I learned later that I was also afraid of success.

When failure is experienced, the therapy process is very important since the patient knows that, other than himself, the therapist is the person who will best understand the situation and will offer encouragement rather than ridicule. Because I was personally programmed for failure, it was very important to me that there was someone who would offer constant assurance that success was a definite possibility for me.

As time passed, I was able to extend my attack on the symptoms of Agoraphobia to more and more experiences. Again, not with total success, but with sufficient positive experiences that I began to feel that I might be symptom-free one day. I was in my third year of therapy at this time. I was a master of all the techniques and personally was amazed at how basic the system was and how well it functioned. We are all like Pavlov's dogs after all. I was able to replace the fear response on entering restaurants and other places of business with my step-by-step new response of confidence and only a slight anxiety. Where before I had been immobilized by anxiety, now I could see it coming and prepare myself to deal with it appropriately. The system was basic and simple and, most importantly, it worked. As I experimented with different situations and with different time sequences, and as I had more successes, I could feel my self-confidence growing. It may seem foolish and difficult to believe that a successful drive downtown, parking the car, and entering a store could be the reason for personal exhilaration and great celebration. But it was! Each event of this kind was progress back to normalcy and away from fear. Sometimes it was hard for even me to realize that I had developed such dread of the normal, everyday aspects of life that I had once wished for death.

Along with this increasing control over my physical activities, I was also gaining control over my inner self.

The small successes I experienced in the real world were translated into a growing confidence in myself as a person. Little by little, I was coming to believe that I was not a failure. In fact, for the first time, I was becoming convinced of my worth as a human being. I was making my way through a private hell to the other side. My hardware of therapy—the techniques of behavior modification were working for me most of the time. In addition to this, the root causes of my illness were, by this time, well understood by my therapist and by me. They were events in time which were part of my personal development and growth. I was stuck with them. Still, in spite of their existence and their manifestation as Agoraphobia, I was finding a way to deal with them. I had to learn a new emotional response to the situations and events and people which had conditioned my behavior in the first place. This type of re-learning was many times more difficult than learning to overcome the fear responses of Agoraphobia. After all, many of the things I was conditioned to as a child were forgotten, or at least buried under years of living. But it was necessary to deal with these early conditions since they were at the bottom of my problems. Unfortunately, there would never be a possibility for me to go back in time and say to my family, "please don't ruin my self-concept or I'll be a failure for the rest of my life. Please accept me as you find me; different from you but, nonetheless, valuable as a human. Celebrate my uniqueness and help me find a way to develop and use my mind." Of course, there is no means by which the direction of past events can now be altered. The only alteration is the situation that is possible in my own personal re-evaluation of my history in the light of my new-found understanding and confidence which I have developed. This aspect of my therapy represented and still does represent the more difficult and complex areas that I have had to deal with. In many ways this stage of the therapy process is an on-going one, perhaps a lifetime effort. As I made my way through the convolutions of my personal psychological development,

I came to see how much the illness of one psyche can illustrate the illness of a whole society. To define what I mean by this statement I can reduce my case to its simplest analysis: had I been born male, or been born at a later time in the twentieth century when females had achieved a more equal status in the society, perhaps I would have had a secure self-image and the symptoms of Agoraphobia would never have emerged. If I had been born into the company of a more tolerant and understanding family and had thereby received some confirmation of my self-worth from these primary people in my life; perhaps then Agoraphobia and I would have never met.

All of these suppositions are based on the premise that Agoraphobia is primarily the result of environmental or life situation experiences. However, at the present time, the etiology of Agoraphobia is the subject of much research. Some of this research is based on the hypothesis that a bio-chemical defect may be the basis of the development of the symptoms we call Agoraphobia. If a bio-chemical defect is the primary cause of Agoraphobia and a person is subjected to the type of life environment described earlier, then the development of Agoraphobia is inevitable. It would be important that not only the bio-chemical problem must be treated, but also the life situation must be free of the type of attacks on the developing individual such as I experienced.

Various ramifications of the question of how Agoraphobia originates will be discussed at length further along in this work. It is important to understand that, as with most human problems, solutions do not come easily nor are they often simple. Agoraphobia represents a difficulty which has many symptoms and probably multiple causes. In the present state of the art of therapy intervention, the judicious use of each method of treatment seems the best course until a definitive answer is found through research.

I have found that society can make it very difficult for those not in the mainstream to function comfortably. When I speak of not being in the mainstream, I am speaking of those individuals whose basic philosophy and value systems may be different from those in the society in which he finds himself, or the society into which he is born. And the society to which he is born begins with the immediate family. Those individuals not in the mainstream comprise the loners, the eccentrics, the political dissidents, and the marginal individuals for whom society has no comfortable niche. Because society is not comfortable with these individuals, society in most cases rejects them. This rejection, which often begins at the family level, is interpreted by the individual to mean he has no worth to others. It is an easy and obvious next step for the individual to develop a sense of low self-worth also. When these events take place, there are certain options open short of self destruction. First is the art of compromise which succeeds well for some people. Second, it is always possible to reject the status quo, drop out and become a member of some counter-culture lifestyle. However, in my case, I chose to opt for compromise and this choice led me to a lifelong confusion and battle within myself. Combining the conditions of compromise with my internal conflicts made fertile ground for the development of emotional illness. Although many people are able to make comfortable adjustments as they compromise this and that throughout their lives, for some reason I was unable to adjust in this way. The reasons are not so obscure looked at from the later understanding I gained of myself through therapy. I know that I interpreted every demand that I conform to my family's codes and conditions, without modification from my own point of view, as an affront to my own personal worth. I was never consulted about my feelings, my ideas, my differences. I was merely expected to absorb the dogma related to me by the senior generations and, of course, I accepted this all, at least overtly. But while I was wearing the mask of obedient acceptance, I was internally rejecting it all. I am sure that if I had experienced some feelings of value about myself, I would not have reacted so strongly to some very superficial and unimportant compromises I came to make as I grew up.

There is no emotional illness which can develop and grow in isolation. In every case there exists important social factors which have augmented its development. In many cases emotional illnesses such as Agoraphobia develop because there is no other outlet for a sick psyche to express itself. Pathological though it may be, the emergence of an emotional illness is a last attempt of a sick ego to express itself and to attempt to deal with the world around it. It is an admission of failure of individual adjustment and it is also the last compromise with the indifference of society. In the case of the development of Agoraphobia as an example of the influence of social factors in the development of emotional illness, it is interesting to study the nature of the symptoms that are characteristic of the problem. Every Agoraphobic shows an extreme amount of fear and anxiety. Although the objects of the fear and the anxiety will be different for different individuals, the fact is that the primary feature is fear and the inability to deal with life on a day-to-day basis. An Agoraphobic is uncomfortable in an environment that is not of his own making. He views the outside world in terms of its hostility and threat. In other words, an Agoraphobic in some manner becomes alienated from the society he is in. He is no longer able to find the rewards that participation in the mainstream gives to the non-Agoraphobic. In the lifetime of each Agoraphobic, there is some crucial point at which he is rejected by a loved one, or by the general society in which he lives. This event may represent the accumulation of many rejections with subsequent damage to the ego, and the result hastens the development of Agoraphobia. Often the precipitating cause of the symptoms is not any one incident or person, but it is the accumulative effects of a lifetime. It is more than the effects of stress that operates in the development of Agoraphobia. Nor is it that Agoraphobics have faulty ego structures from the beginning which might predispose them to the illness. The critical set of conditions which can produce Agoraphobic behavior include an ego which has been unduly worn down by too much compromise, too much criticism, both from self and others.

There is a personality characteristic which Agoraphobics share and which is important also. That characteristic is a compulsive desire to please, or at the very least not to offend, those around him. This characteristic operates with the Agoraphobic's use of compromise to result in an outwardly pleasing, compliant personality, whose natural hostility or anger is always suppressed.

From societal expectations and from early family training, the Agoraphobic has learned his lesson well and has continued to practice what is learned throughout his life. In the case of a female Agoraphobic, by complying with the expectations of others all her life, she has been her own worst enemy. It is no surprise that the ratio of female to male Agoraphobics is 9 to 1. It has always been more difficult for a female to express non-traditional behavior or non-conventional ideas than for a male to do the same. Family and societal expectations for the female have been more stereotyped and historically most women have conformed to these controls and have conformed to the stereotype. In doing so, many individuals have sacrificed certain aspects of their own personal development. Women, particularly, have postponed their career desires or personal development to the demands of homemaking and child raising. This represents the conforming role that meets family and societal expectations. It is also the easier role to assume. With this in mind, the typical Agoraphobic could be characterized as a young married woman, often with a family to take care of. Suddenly, one day she finds herself unable to do the family shopping at the grocery store, or driving to school to pick up the children fills her with dread. Perhaps the first panic attack comes when she is shopping with a friend in a department store and she finds she cannot bring herself to enter the elevator. She makes an excuse and after a time puts the incident from her mind. But each time she thinks about elevators she is aware of the stressing symptoms of anxiety. Symptoms such as those described here and earlier can appear in anyone at any time but for the prospective Agoraphobic, the symptoms increase and become constant to the point of controlling his life—or to be more accurate, her life. While this is taking place in her life, there is no neat, logical course of events which could be observed at some point and interrupted so that Agoraphobia could be prevented. In fact, in some cases, the progress of the problem is so slow and insidious that it is difficult to pinpoint where and when and how the symptoms began to emerge. Sometimes neurotic symptoms develop as part of a growth process right along with the normal growth and development of an individual. Research would probably show that female children who are thwarted in their natural development; that is, female children who are denied the prerogative of making choices which may be outside the conventional, societal role, have a good chance of developing a neurosis later on in life and that neurosis will likely present the symptoms of Agoraphobia. In analytical terms, Agoraphobia is merely the configuration of symptoms and behavior which indicate a basic ego identity conflict. In simple terms, there is a difference between the perceived me and the real me. The problem arises because a very caring and conforming individual has grown up catering to the wishes and standards of family and society to such an extent that the basic underlying personality is in conflict with the facade personality which has developed throughout the years. The basic conflict has always been present but was not consciously acknowledged until some critical experience or event causes some symptoms to become obvious. Depending upon individual circumstances, a fully developed and disabling neurosis may take extended time to become evident, but, eventually, if the conflict is not resolved, Agoraphobia will appear.

It is interesting to speculate that because of the new

and better position of women in society, future years should show a decrease in the number of cases of Agoraphobia and a better and earlier diagnosis of the cases that do arise.

There is another aspect to the diagnosis and treatment of Agoraphobia which I have not dealt with in discussing my own case or the study of Agoraphobia in general. That neglected aspect is depression. In addition to the other symptoms which I have described at length, depression appears to be a key factor in the development of Agoraphobia. Viewed from one perspective, it seems that the constant presence of fear and anxiety combined with the extreme effort put forth to deal with them could reasonably be expected to produce depression in anyone. However in analyzing my own life experience and comparing it with others, it becomes clear that a lifelong serious state of depression has been a part of or preceded the development of Agoraphobia rather than developing as a result of it. It is important to make this distinction when understanding depression and Agoraphobia. If the development of the symptoms of Agoraphobia is one type of response to environmental stresses acting on a bio-chemical defect, it must be conceded that the bio-chemical defect came first. In the research currently being done (as mentioned earlier), the bio-chemical problem appears to involve depressions, a condition which pre-dates the onset of the symptoms of Agoraphobia. Treatment of this condition with anti-depressant drug therapy has been every effective in not only reducing the depression but in also lessening the anxiety and panic of the Agoraphobia.

When discussing depression, I am not speaking of the common depression that is the natural and appropriate response to a life situation. In such cases, it is obvious that having feelings of depression is completely understandable. There is the knowledge that given the necessary passage of time or a change in life situation, the depression will pass and other feelings will become dominant over the depression again. However, in the case of chronic, clinical depression, which is the type associated with Agoraphobia, there are two important differences: First the presence of feelings of depression is not due to any life condition which would normally call for depression as a response. In fact, the depression seems to be attached to no one particular event or circumstance. Instead it is a general response to everything. This type of depression is a continuous state of feeling that to a greater or lesser extent is part of every feeling, thought, and action that the victim is part of. In much the same way that the fear response in Agoraphobia becomes generalized, so that behavior is altered, depression becomes generalized so that feelings are altered. The individual may put a good face on things so that his true feelings go undetected but underlying all is a condition of unrelenting depression which mutes and modifies every other emotional state. As it functions in Agoraphobia, the depression is highlighted as the Agoraphobic experiences fear reactions or failures in his experiences. These circumstances lead to more depression and the grim cycle is set up—depression, failure and more depression. As long as the underlying causes for the original state of depression are not dealt with, no amount of behavior modification will remove the symptoms of recurring depression.

To further complicate the understanding of the basic depression state underlying Agoraphobia, it is only necessary to recall that one of the significant characteristics of an Agoraphobic is that his behavior is often dictated by the expectations of others. Since sadness or depression is a sure way to drive others away, particularly if it is persistent, the Agoraphobic does everything in his power to convince himself and others that he is not depressed. This has been a lifetime deception on his part and he may even believe himself when he claims that he is not depressed. If we accept the hypothesis that Agoraphobia is symptomatic of an ego identity conflict, then it might also be hypothesized that such a conflict, nurtured over a lifetime, could produce chronic depression. As noted earlier, the symptoms and behavior of Agoraphobics could very obviously produce feelings of hopelessness in anyone plus a feeling of despair at ever being able to change anything. Depression feeds on such a state of affairs. Practitioners of the technique of behavior modification are extremely helpful in dealing with the many fear symptoms and in teaching techniques of re-directing behavior in those ways which help the Agoraphobic to function in his life situation with a lesser amount of dis-comfort. In spite of its success in these areas, behavior modification techniques are not too useful in altering the effects of depression. While it is beneficial to have a lessen-ing of the symptoms and a feeling of control of oneself again, through the use of behavior modification, it is, at the same time, frustrating to experience the continuing presence of depression. What this means is that the full enjoyment of life is still one step removed from the Agoraphobic and will remain in that position until his depression is dealt with in some way.

I personally became aware of the intensity of my own depression when I was well along in my second year of ther-apy. I began to notice that no matter how successful I felt as I mastered one symptom after the other, there was still something missing. My relief at being able to do things on my own and with others was real enough but whether from habit or whatever, I could feel no lasting elation at my prog-ress. There was one factor which caused me concern as I progressed along with my weekly therapy sessions, and that was my uncontrollable crying during the session. Tears would come over me as I would begin to talk about certain sub-jects with my therapist. It was not a case of sobbing or a good cry but rather just unwanted tears. Between wiping my eyes and nose, I managed to keep talking. Sometimes I would deliberately try to change the subject when I felt my crying was interfering with my ability to communicate. I was often at a loss to understand exactly what subject matter seemed to overwhelm me so. During these times, my thera-pist would ask me exactly what I thought the tears meant.

84

I was never able to find a very satisfactory answer, perhaps because there were many answers. I believe I cried for myself and what I believed was a wasted life. I also cried out of anger, the kind of anger that was always hidden from others in my attempt or need to be "acceptable." Behavioral scientists believe that anger and hostility are components of depression.

The Agoraphobic who suffers most of the time in silence and hides his symptoms from others and even from himself, inevitably has anger and hostility as part of his hidden feelings. Because he has tried so hard throughout his life to suppress these feelings, they become covert aspects of his depression.

In my earlier therapy sessions I was able to get in touch with some of my long repressed feelings, but for some time I was not able to articulate the ideas and experiences that were a part of those feelings. To have such intense emotional expressions and not to be able to understand where these emotions were coming from was frustrating and, in a sense, terrifying. Many times I half believed that I had experienced some dreadful event in my life which I had afterwards repressed and the tears and depression were the only conscious memory that I retained. Unfortunately, or fortunately, I was never able to discover any one event which lay at the foundation of my problems. But I did learn many things about depression and how it is related to Agoraphobia.

As personal conflicts develop, from whatever cause, and the individual loses ego strength and self-esteem, it becomes easy to withdraw from society and to retreat into a private, safe world. Viewed from this perspective, the Agoraphobic's symptoms make logical sense. Since he is depressed with the general state of his life for reasons not clearly understood, he finds a method of withdrawing from life or from participating in the usual functions of living. He sees himself as no longer successful in competing in the mainstream of life and he begins to exhibit behavioral changes

85

which he cannot explain and by which he becomes victimized. All of this adds to his original depression. As the Agoraphobic finds himself less and less comfortable in certain situations, he becomes absorbed in his own private world of depression and fear.

The condition of depression has had a good body of research devoted to its causes and cures because it is not only an important component of Agoraphobia, but it is also often present in other emotional problems. It is important to be aware of the distinction between everyday transient depression and what is called endogenous depression, or a depression which originates internally. For the layman, depression is difficult to deal with because everyone has had some experience with its symptoms and everyone is willing and ready to offer private advice concerning how it should be handled. From the perspective of the depressed person, nothing seems as hollow or cruel as the recommendation to "snap out of it" or "find an activity to get your mind off yourself." If the cure for depression were that simple, depressed feelings would practically never rise to the surface and overwhelm the victim. It is absurd to offer such advice to an Agoraphobic with depression or to anyone suffering with endogenous depression. If a pep talk, a change of activity, or success in overcoming some of the symptoms of Agoraphobia will not help rid a person of his depression, then what will help?

Current trends in research seem to favor an electrochemical or bio-chemical factor in the brain as important in understanding depression. Certain drugs have been developed which help to control the more troublesome aspects of depression in most cases. These anti-depressant drugs keep the feelings of depression within the ability of the person to handle without interfering with normal functioning. In the particular case of the person who is both depressed and Agoraphobic, the use of anti-depressant drugs can be most helpful when they are used in conjunction with other forms of therapy. When used with behavior modification techniques for instance, the effect of the anti-depressant is to reduce the effect of any failure that might be experienced while working through the behavioral changes in an anxiety producing situation. If an Agoraphobic is struggling with the problem of entering a busy supermarket to do the weekly shopping, and finds herself in a panic attack when she tries to accomplish her goal, the subsequent depression of failure only adds to the general feelings associated with a poor self-image and the original depression she is trying to overcome. Using an anti-depressant drug provides a cushion so that the new depression will not make the entire situation too overwhelming to be endured.

Anti-depressants are not "uppers" in the sense that they produce feelings of euphoria or elation. The effect that they have is to bring the feelings into normal range or to stabilize the depressed person so that any day-to-day depression associated with life in general will be handled in a suitable context. The use of anti-depressants in the treatment of Agoraphobia is not a cure-all by any means. The fact that they have any effect at all is significant in trying to understand what combinations of factors can help cure mental and emotional illness. It is becoming obvious that the answers to the problems posed by such illnesses are as complex as the questions. Research into brain chemistry has helped to produce such chemical aids as the anti-depressant drugs but it is not clear at this writing why the drugs are effective in some cases and not in others. It is possible that there are chemical deficiencies in the brain itself which are genetic and which drugs are able to help only partially. Another aspect of the entire problem of brain chemistry is the way in which a chemical defect in the brain can become evident as a change in an individual's behavior. In the case of the development of Agoraphobia, there seems to be a straight line relationship between lifelong endogenous depression and the development of the symptoms of Agoraphobia. As has been noted, this combination of events is particularly lethal for females. When the pressures of society and family and the probability of role conflict are added in, a bright and sensitive female who tries to challenge the status quo will likely end up with the symptoms of Agoraphobia. Many intriguing questions arise from a consideration of the factors which enter into the process. For example, does the problem exist in other cultures where the role of the female may be differently defined? Has the new and changing status of women had any effect on the incidence of Agoraphobia among women? Is there a genetic or hormonal or experiential difference in women that could account for the higher incidence of the problem in that sex? With the changing role of the female, there is a concomitant change for the male also. Since this is the case, can we expect an increasing number of cases of Agoraphobia among men? All of these are questions for future research, obviously, and in the meantime, the victims of Agoraphobia must use every system and aid now available to help overcome the paralyzing effects of the symptoms. The anti-depressant drugs are certainly one of the more helpful aids at the present time. I have found, in my own case, that utilizing all the available helps simultaneously has been the most successful and beneficial. If it were possible for the anti-depressants to remove or to mask all the depression, and if it were possible for the behavior modification techniques to change things completely for the Agoraphobic so that there would be no more irrational fears and that no behavioral relapses could be expected, then curing Agoraphobia would be simple. Because the above conditions do not prevail at this time, the possibility or probability of an Agoraphobic becoming symptom-free is not a reasonable expectation. What is reasonable to expect is that an Agoraphobic can gain mastery over the symptoms and an understanding of why and how they came about. To arrive at this place means a continuous process of self-exploration and self-understanding combined with the sheer guts to overcome the disability.

CHAPTER V

Two further aspects of my personal struggle with Agoraphobia are worth taking note of since my experiences would most probably be similar to those of other Agoraphobics.

The most amazing and in some ways discouraging aspect of seeking professional help was the discovery that many, if not most, psychologists and psychiatrists have only a cursory understanding of Agoraphobia. Since it has always been classified with all the other phobias, there has been no attempt by the professions to consider it as a complex of symptoms or as a syndrome. It is unfortunate that this neurosis has been misunderstood historically. Treating it as merely another phobic condition will miss understanding the magnitude of the problem and the importance of using more than one method in attempting a cure. To be fair to the professions, it has to be remembered that because of the nature of the problem few Agoraphobics are ever seen in the offices of therapists. If a therapist is consulted, the Agoraphobia could easily be missed and the complex of symptoms would be placed under the general diagnosis of anxiety. As mentioned earlier, the standard prescription for anxiety states is tranquilizers. In most cases, using tranquilizers merely postpones the necessary dealings with the underlying problem of Agoraphobia. Many of the effects of the tranquilizers add to the depression which already exists. Put another way, these drugs remove the person one more distance from his feelings. The occasional use of tranquilizers or alcohol to help with an acute anxiety attack may work very well but there is no substitute for good therapy and proper medication.

I have noted that it has been historically difficult for Agoraphobics to get as far as the therapist's office, consequently, few therapists have ever treated an Agoraphobic. In recent years, however, some behavior modification "clinics" have been started, especially in California. Often both the Agoraphobic and spouse or partner attend these clinics and practice the techniques of behavior modification therapy together. They have practice sessions together so that the Agoraphobic can come to feel that the partner is a safe and understanding person who will understand and help in anxiety producing situations. The Agoraphobic learns that he can leave a problem area if things become too difficult and that he can practice again without feeling guilty at having failed the first time. Under this format of behavior modification, there is an expectation that the Agoraphobic can learn a new response to a situation that has proven to be too intimidating for him before. He practices the experience with the "safe" partner until confidence is built again and the situation is no longer threatening. Later he will try the same exercise alone using the techniques he has learned with his partner which have helped him. There is no guarantee that even after long praactice and many good experiences that there will be no recurrences of the anxiety symptoms. Nothing so far can suggest a one hundred percent cure for Agoraphobics. However, the important thing is that by using all the means available to help, Agoraphobics can and do become more independent and more able to live a near-normal life without undue stress or panic attacks. There is another gain in learning how to use the techniques of behavior modification and desensitization with a partner. That additional gain is that the partner also becomes a part of the cure and develops a better understanding of what Agoraphobics have to contend with. Many times this new understanding makes the difference between losing a relationship and saving it in spite of one party having Agoraphobia. Just as life becomes miserable for the Agoraphobic, it can also become trying for members of his family or living partners. Many times the other members of the household have tried for years to understand the behavior of the Agoraphobic, but because it is too difficult for the Agoraphobic to communicate about his problem to anyone, a conspiracy of silence develops and everyone suffers. Behavior modification can bring about remarkable changes that are observable to everyone and for that reason it is more than useful for the Agoraphobic to understand and practice its techniques. It is a sure way for the self-image to improve too, because seeing your own progress is its own reward. The one question as yet unanswered is whether the good early results of the application of behavior modification techniques in the elimination of the symptoms of Agoraphobia will last over time. This, too, awaits the results of further research and is under study.

In addition to drugs and behavior modification, there is the area of individual and/or group therapy available to help the Agoraphobic. I have been involved in a self-help group situation for about two years, along with my own individual psychotherapy. There is great comfort in knowing there are others who have the same difficulty and problems in dealing with a life encumbered by Agoraphobia. Meeting once a week to exchange ideas, feelings and successes has great value in adding some continuity as well as sociability to life.

There is one obvious difficulty in the self-help group idea for Agoraphobics and that is attendance. For the same reason few therapists ever treat an Agoraphobic (because of the problems involved in getting to the office), it is often difficult to convince them that attending a group meeting can be beneficial. For those who do manage this task, however, the results are worth the effort.

Psychotherapy on an individual basis can be very expensive and very time-consuming. Often there are long periods when nothing productive seems to be happening. The probing which is a part of the therapy process can, itself, become threatening and lead to a revival of symptoms and a feeling of frustration over ever coming to grips with causes, let alone cures. But in order to understand and perhaps prevent the occurrence of Agoraphobia, it is necessary for some of its victims to look beyond the behavioral aspects of the problem and allow their lives to be examined in an effort to find those factors which lead to its development in the first place. It is only through individual therapy that this kind of understanding can come about. On the other hand, group therapy, from my personal experience at least, is not the best method for treating Agoraphobia. Groups which are made up of only Agoraphobics, such as those which exist in a clinic setting, have been successful with the use of behavior modification systems. Within this group setting, Agoraphobics seem to understand and help one another. On the other hand, in a group setting where the participants present more varied problems, it is sometimes difficult for an Agoraphobic to make himself and his illness understood by the group. Depending upon the severity of the symptoms and the individual's life situation, almost any form of treatment is preferred over trying to exist with no professional help at all. For myself, it has always been essential to have an understanding of not only my illness, but also the dynamics of how I ever developed it.

After a period of three years during which most of my therapy was concerned with trying to help me overcome my symptoms so that I could begin to live a more normal life again, I felt I needed to go on to a more comprehensive knowledge of myself and my problem. This led me to a therapist with a more analytical approach.

As I have written here many times, there is no one hundred percent guarantee, that even under the best circumstances, there will not be some recurrence of symptoms; some periods of high anxiety and panic. However, I finally learned that even when these difficult times occur, I am familiar with their course and I am able to deal with their presence rather than take flight in fear. I understand that I may never be free of symptoms completely, but the progress I have made personally has given me back my confidence, so that I can tolerate what I cannot change. It has been through the aid of analytical therapy that I have come to the strong conviction that Agoraphobia is a complex condition requiring the administration of more than one type of therapy. In order to understand its dynamics in any individual case, it becomes necessary to explore the family and childhood and adolescent background of the Agoraphobic. If the patient is a woman, and it usually is, the probability of some sort of ego identity or role conflict problem is likely as I have noted. This aspect is not always obvious to the patient and it may take considerable probing to discover its dynamics.

Depression is a major factor in Agoraphobia and where medication can alleviate some of its discomfort, the professions should use it. Just because depression is a factor in many other emotional and mental illnesses, it should not be assumed that it has only a minor role in the development of Agoraphobia. I am convinced that had I not pursued the possibility of there being something physically wrong with me so that I was finally given anti-depressants, I would never have overcome so many of my symptoms, regardless of how much behavior modification therapy I practiced. I would have spent my life dealing with my symptoms with no clear understanding of how they originated and that they could have a physiological basis. I was fortunate because I had a working knowledge of human behavior plus an interest in medicine so that I was able to suggest to my doctor that I was suffering from more than a behavioral problem. It took some shopping among physicians to find one who was willing to accept my hypothesis. It is not my intention to indict the healing professions. Dealing in human behavior is an obscure area. But it is important for those afflicted with Agoraphobia to understand that they may have to press the professions for a more thorough investigation of their individual problem. It will often be necessary for these non-assertive Agoraphobic women to take the initiative where their own emotional and physical well-being is concerned. Where a combination of therapy and drugs is indicated, neither should be neglected just because traditional professional opinion has preferred one form of treatment over another. Many times it is necessary to shop for a therapist with an eclectic approach. This circumstance places the Agoraphobic in a very difficult position since the shopping only adds to his anxiety if he has to go from doctor to doctor. It is to be hoped that as research progresses and more definitive information is developed concerning Agoraphobia, the victims will be able to find help more easily.

Part of the body of information that needs to be gathered to further research will be developed from those Agoraphobics who are willing to have their personal lives explored in some depth. It is only from this type of data that some conclusions may be drawn concerning the important question of why Agoraphobia develops and why most of its victims are women. Because Agoraphobia has been a hidden illness for so long, there may be a built-in resistance to revealing personal details by those who have it. An interesting fact has been noted by those few who have studied several cases of Agoraphobia. There are apparently many similarities in the life background and experiences of Agoraphobics regardless of age, lifestyle, socio-economic status, etc. There is a shared history as well as the shared experience of having Agoraphobia. A key question for research is what is the interrelationship between being Agoraphobic and having certain personality characteristics which are shared in common? Since there has been little experience with the condition on the part of professionals, or contact among victims themselves, there must be some explanation other than learned behavior which accounts for the evidence of common features. Besides research into brain chemistry, all other correlates of the problem must be discovered and understood and to do this will require the willingness of Agoraphobic individuals to be studied in depth.

Agoraphobia presents a challenge to the professions since it obviously involves physical, psychological and sociological aspects and a unique interrelationship among them. From experience, it is clear to me personally that the treatment of any one dimension to the exclusion of the others cannot be successful. The inclusiveness of the problem demands a multi-dimensioned approach. In addition to this challenge to the professions, the Agoraphobic himself needs to be made aware of his individual responsibility to educate his family and friends about Agoraphobia so that awareness of the problem is promoted throughout society.

There is always solace for a victim in learning that a problem he thought was his alone turns out to be shared by many more than he could ever know. Agoraphobics can gain this solace by helping to promote information and understanding about their problem to those around them. This is an assignment not easily undertaken. For an Agoraphobic, whose entire life has been given over to secrecy and subterfuge concerning his problem, to suddenly open up to others is asking for real courage. But it will take this sort of personal, individual commitment of self-revelation before any real understanding can follow. It is up to those who have this problem to aid in promoting its understanding, research and eventual cure.

One means of sharing the problems of Agoraphobia is by forming local support groups of Agoraphobics who can help one another. This help may be in the form of a telephone call of reassurance from time to time, or a visit to a home-bound member. Supporting and helping one another to function in the real world is another way Agoraphobics can share their mutual problems. The idea that Agoraphobics can even consider forming themselves into support groups and attending meetings may sound absurd at first thought. But as noted earlier, where this has been tried, it has proved very successful for many people.

In an effort to test this idea for myself, I and a fellow Agoraphobic initiated the formation of a support group for Agoraphobics in California. We began with some realistic assumptions that have proven to be valid: 1) Agoraphobics are shy and fearful of being identified. 2) The motivation to do something to help oneself is difficult to find in an Agoraphobic. 3) The practical aspect of getting Agoraphobics out of their homes is almost insurmountable, especially since one of the most common difficulties is the inability to drive. Despite these and other obstacles, the good effect of the support group justifies trying to overcome the difficulties.

After the group spent a few one or two hour sessions with one another, it was noticeable that individual anxiety was lessening as the members became acquainted with each other and began to trust the situation. This sort of reaction was not universal, of course. For some people, any exchange of information about Agoraphobia can be felt as threatening. In these cases, we encouraged them to attend for as long a period as possible and to leave whenever they felt uncomfortable. Experience with support groups has shown that if the individual remains with the group for a sufficiently long period, he will find that any build-up of anxiety from conversation about the problem will soon diminish. In fact, there will eventually be a security found in the group situation and the members will vie with one another for speaking rights.

A support group is very different from a therapy group or group therapy. In a support group, the main idea is to understand one another and to feel comfortable because there are others who have shared or are sharing the same experience. It is particularly true in the case of Agoraphobia, that the realization that the problem is not limited to you alone has an almost instant effect for the better. Countless times I have seen the look of relief appear on the faces of group members when they realize that they are in a room filled with others who have gone through the same terrors and have had occasion to doubt their sanity also.

Another advantage of having a support group for Agoraphobics is purely practical. It is easier to practice the techniques of behavior modification by using a group member as a "safe person" rather than relying on a non-Agoraphobic partner. The factor of understanding that one group member brings to another insures that explanations for Agoraphobic behavior need not be made endlessly, nor are failures criticized. We have used this buddy system successfully with our support group. The individual who can drive a car comfortably provides transportation for the person who is not able to drive. The person who has conquered the supermarket fears helps another to desensitize to the supermarket. After a period of individual practice, the support group members each report on their progress at the next meeting. This exchange of experiences is beneficial whether the experience was a success or a failure. Many useful hints are exchanged and just knowing that others are trying to overcome the same difficulties is a positive element in keeping up enthusiasm.

In addition to the meetings and the practice together, a support group may also set up a telephone network so that contact with an understanding member is always available. One other important aspect of a support group for Agoraphobics that needs mentioning is the obvious benefits of socialization. In many cases, especially where the Agoraphobia is of long standing, social contacts have been limited or restricted to immediate family members. The support group offers a change from this routine and its members can become friends with one another. The group offers an opportunity to practice social skills which may have been neglected and to practice without fear of ridicule regardless of the behavior. Overall, the concept of support groups for Agoraphobics is a theoretically sound and practically expedient means of self-help. It is not a substitute for individual therapy but it is very useful as an adjunct to therapy and has the effect of helping the Agoraphobic out of his prison.

CHAPTER VI

Since beginning to write about my experience with Agoraphobia, I have been through another year and one-half of psychotherapy. The focus for this period of time has been on the dynamics of my personal life as it is concerned with the development of Agoraphobia. I have learned much about my personal case. Some of what I have discovered probably has general applicability to others with the problem or, at least, the information could offer some insight when there was none before. As I have stated elsewhere in this writing, individual life circumstances will obviously vary with the individual Agoraphobic. However, this does not preclude the presence of definite similarities in experience which need to be understood when trying to deal with the problem of Agoraphobia. By investigating my own life and the development of my Agoraphobia and then exchanging information with group members, I have come to these conclusions:

1. Agoraphobia probably begins to develop in childhood, but is not usually manifest until age twenty to thirty, and sometimes later.

2. The onset of symptoms often coincides with a traumatic experience either physical or psychological.

3.	In spite of the fact that the early symptoms are confined to one or two situations, eventually the symptoms will generalized to other areas making it impossible to function in a normal manner.

4.	It is important at this stage of knowledge to combine forms of treatment in order to achieve the best results. For some people overcoming the symptoms through the use of behavior modification techniques may seem to be sufficient, but it is doubtful the changes will be lasting without some form of insight into the root causes.

5.	There are definite indications that the reason more women than men present the symptoms of Agoraphobia is due partly to family and societal pressures early in their developmental years.

6.	The helping professions, psychiatry and psychology, have been remiss in not becoming knowledgeable about Agoraphobia, in often mis-diagnosing the problem, or of being unaware of its existence for so long a period. It is true that, in the past, few Agoraphobics found their way to professional offices due to the nature of their problem. However, now that more is being understood about the problem, it is important that it be understood as a complex syndrome and should not be treated as merely another of the phobias. The lives and talents that have been lost to years of Agoraphobic isolation are testimony to the need for adequate treatment and ultimately prevention of the condition.

Agoraphobia presents implications for society as a whole, particularly where the position of women is concerned. Every institution within the social structure must come to the awareness that there is no difference between the needs of male and female egos for recognition. Stereotyping for either sex is archaic; opportunities for either sex must be the same. This means family opportunities, educational opportunities, and social and economic opportunities. Those who study such things know that there is a definite relationship between feelings of personal alienation and attitudes of social alienation. In the case of Agoraphobia it is clear that the personal alienation which may be one of the basic influences in developing the condition, leads directly to increased social alienation as the Agoraphobic retreats further and further from contacts with the world. No one is more aware of the feelings of being apart from the mainstream of life than an Agoraphobic who has spent a decade or two living a hidden, lonely existence.

Out of this consideration, one question begs for an answer: Can psychological illness be due to a failure of society as a whole to really meet individual needs? The burden of failure to meet these needs falls on everyone ultimately in the form of increased crime, physical illness, mental and emotional illness. It is easy to meet needs and to provide opportunities when an individual conforms or potentially conforms to the status quo. Casting each generation in the mold of its predecessor is self-validating and comfortable. But the traditional roles that families and societies have provided for each generation are proving to be too rigid and narrowly defined. Human rights must henceforth include the right to be different, while at the same time having the right to be successful and valued by society. The high drama of the individual who triumphs over adversity and blends into the common landscape must be realistically understood for the myth that it is. The stress of the challenge of being different probably defeats ten times more people than those who rise above it. To value uniqueness in an individual means loving and encouraging a child who shows his family that he sees himself in a different setting with different goals. He needs to believe that he is still loved and appreciated by those whose life he shares. To disapprove of individuality in a child is to condemn him to self-doubt and personal chaos later as an adult. For parents to try to find through their children some sort of personal mirror image of themselves, or to live out some frustration through the accomplishments of their children, is to place a heavy burden from one generation upon another. Each of us is his own assemblage and should be judged only within his individual context.

Out of the therapy, self-examination and personal contact I have had with others who have Agoraphobia, I have developed a new appreciation of the strength of the human need to endure. I have come from a frightened existence to a near full life. I have found a validation for myself in seeing others who are like me. I have come from the position of no conviction of the value of therapy to a sincere advocacy of its merits. It would be naive to expect a badly damaged psyche to emerge completely new and whole from the insights developed through therapy, but for many the reward of reclaiming oneself is enough. In the end, perhaps what can be said for the therapy process is that two minds are brought together for the purpose of proscribing a route for one of them which has the least amount of convolutions compatible with its capacity to endure.

EPILOGUE

Throughout this work, I have stressed the value of combining forms of therapy because a multi-dimensional approach to the problems of Agoraphobia would assure the best results in terms of a "cure." The results of current research suggests modification of this point of view. Or perhaps clarification is the better word.

There is one area of therapy which has always been controversial and that is the use of drug therapy in the treatment of Agoraphobia. As more and more data is accumulated through research studies, the results are more definitive in suggesting that at the root of the problem of Agoraphobia lies a bio-chemical defect, probably genetic in origin. It is more accurate to state that at the root of the problem of depression is a bio-chemical defect. Since we have already established the fact that depression is not only a part of Agoraphobia, but is probably the fundamental cause of its symptoms, by inference it is assumed that at the root of Agoraphobia is a bio-chemical problem. It appears that any successful or sustained treatment of Agoraphobia must include the application of drug therapy as well as other methods.

Using behavior modification techniques or exposure therapy in the treatment of Agoraphobia has proven to be of utmost value in desensitizing and providing a method of meeting the demands of everyday living such as socializing, shopping, traveling, etc. But just as behavioral change therapy is not sufficient when used exclusively, neither is medication a complete remedy, at least at this time.

The use of medication is, however, less and less controversial and contemporary research studies show the value of anti-depressant drugs in overcoming the symptoms of depression and anxiety. One class of these drugs (the MAO inhibitors) has proven specifically useful in treating Agoraphobia. It is clear from these studies that in order for any form of therapy to be effective, treatment of the bio-chemical aspect of the problem must be included in the approach. Combining the various methods of therapy requires a rather sophisticated understanding of the various effects of different types of therapy and their individual and combined effectiveness in meeting the problem. Not many therapists can meet these standards of chemical and behavioral knowledge but more are learning about those areas in which they are deficient. In the meantime, those who have Agoraphobia must make themselves aware of the many available techniques to help them and they must help one another to seek out all available assistance.

It is not easy to confront a professional and, in effect, do your own diagnosing and even your own prescribing. But for Agoraphobics, this assertive approach is necessary. It may provoke an attitude of hostility on the part of the doctor, and it may be that further searching for the right professional may be necessary. As noted earlier, this searching can mean extra stress for the Agoraphobic, but in some instances it is the only way help can be found. A professional who is comfortable in his own abilities will not be threatened by a patient who wants to inform as well as be helped.

There is an additional means by which one Agoraphobic can help another. If there is a good experience with a doctor for one person, it would be very helpful to share his name with a self-help group or another Agoraphobic. It would not be the intent to flood one doctor's practice with

Agoraphobics, but usually if a professional understands a problem and is interested in it, he will have a colleague who might share his interest and could be persuaded to take on some Agoraphobic patients also. In the group setting in which I have participated, this type of sharing has taken place and has proven very helpful.

One matter of potential controversy must be discussed and that is the subject of professional objections to the use of any medication. Some psychologists, particularly those whose bias is behaviorism, believe that the symptoms of Agoraphobia can be handled through the application of behavior modivication techniques and other behaviorist methods. As I have stated in this work, the use of these techniques to aid in ameliorating the behavioral symptoms which are part of Agoraphobia is without peer as far as results are concerned. Behavior modification, or exposure therapy, is necessary to overcome the poor learning or negative behavioral habits which Agoraphobia causes. Learning the basic technique of desensitization is an absolute necessity if the Agoraphobic is to normalize his behavior and learn to function comfortably. In any form of therapy program, behavior modifying systems should be an additional factor in the plan. But in the case of Agoraphobia, behavioral change is not the only consideration. The results of current research indicate beyond question that there is a bio-chemical component of Agoraphobia. In light of this more current knowledge, it is imperative that drug therapy be combined with behavior modification in order for either approach to be maximally successful. Professional orientation or treatment bias must not interfere with offering the best help available for the Agoraphobic. As a practical matter, cooperation between professionals is often the easiest wasy to resolve a difference in procedure. A psychologist can assure greater success in working with an Agoraphobic by using a cooperating physician or psychiatrist to prescribe and monitor the necessary medication for the patient. With this cooperating effort, the results of therapy will be greatest for the patient, and each professional retains his own area of professional skill.

The use of drug therapy (with the exception of tranquilizers) is not extensively promoted in the case of Agoraphobics because little is understood of the exact way in which they act to affect anxiety and panic. Those professionals who do recognize their value and prescribe them more or less routinely have had success in overcoming not only the symptoms of depression but also in observing a lessening of anxiety and panic attacks.

Understanding the relationship between depression as a bio-chemical problem and the symptoms of Agoraphobia as a behavioral problem is not a simple matter. The interrelationship among chemistry, behavior, and drugs or medication is a complex triad. How is it possible to go from biochemically caused depression to behavior which routinely includes high anxiety and panic attacks, with irrational fears and withdrawal from active participation in life? Exactly what is the connection between depression and Agoraphobia?

Using the bio-chemical model of depression, it is possible to hypothesize the following relationship between depression and Agoraphobia:

Anxiety is a part of depression, anxiety is also a part of fear. The depression which precedes the Agoraphobic symptoms of anxiety, fear, and panic, in effect robs the individual of his reserves, both physical and psychological, and of the energies needed to overcome situational and anticipatory anxiety and fear. Instead of a normal, nontraumatic reaction to a situation, the Agoraphobic whose reserves are depleted, responds in a neurotic manner to a neutral situation with fear and anxiety, thus setting up a response which is negative and which becomes reinforced each time the situation is met again. Because fear and anxiety are strong emotions, they are also strong reinforcers. When combined with depression which has pre-dated the experience, the traumatic effects of experiencing a bizarre reaction to a neutral situation, adds more anxiety and depression to that which already exists. The cycle is then complete with depression, Agoraphobic reactions of anxiety, fear, panic and more depression.

The solution to this problem is then the obvious one of interrupting the cycle at some point so that the depression and the Agoraphobic syndrome no longer interact. As has been discussed here, it is possible to change behavior via modification techniques and thereby alter the cycle. This is appropriate but has its limitations.

A more direct and often faster method of altering depressive, Agoraphobic behavior is to intervene chemically and to help the depression by the use of anti-depressant medication. Using drug therapy can produce dramatic changes in the depression experienced by Agoraphobics. In addition to removing many of the symptoms of depression, the anti-depressant therapy also has a positive affect on Agoraphobia. This seems to happen as a result of the process just described which links depression and Agoraphobia, working in reverse. By lessening the effects of the depression, through the use of anti-depressant drugs, more physical and psychological energy is made available so that the symptoms of Agoraphobia are secondarily affected and controlled, and behavior becomes near normal. This combining of the two therapies, drug intervention and behavior modification, produces the highest probability that improvement will take place.

Because the mechanism involved is very complex and not fully understood at this time, it is only by hypothesis or inference that something like the above sequence may take place between Agoraphobia and depression.

The mechanism which is better understood is how anti-depressant drugs act bio-chemically to reduce depression. How this change takes place is also based upon a hypothesis called the "amine hypothesis of depression." The central thesis of the pathophysiological mechanism of depression theory is that mood states are related to norepinephrine levels at the synapses of brain systems. Depleted levels of norepinephrine result in depression. There is more than norepinephrine involved in the bio-chemical mechanism of depression, but it is used as an illustration of what happens. The actual bio-chemical effect takes place at the synapse. Levels of norephinephrine are available in a "pool" at a nerve ending. At a time of stimulation of a nerve, some of the norepinephrine crosses the synapse to a receptor cell where there are norepinephrine receptor sites. In the case of some depressions, there is a deficiency of this and other amines at the receptor sites in the brain.

In order for there to be an increased supply of norepinephrine available at the receptor sites and thus reduce depression, there must be a chemical mechanism to allow for the release of more norepinephrine from the available pool across the synapse to the receptor. There is such a mechanism and its action forms the basis for the effectiveness of anti-depressant medication. Anti-depressants generally act by inhibiting one chemical so that another (in this case, norepinephrine) can be released and utilized to counter depression. There are two types of anti-depressant drugs, the tricyclic anti-depressants and the monoamine oxidase inhibitors. These drugs act by different means to achieve the effect of altering brain chemistry, but their purpose is the same—to combat depression. The tricyclics (TCAs) are used more frequently since their side effects are less difficult to manage than are the side effects which develop when monamine oxidase inhibitors (MAOIs) are used. There are also certain diet restrictions associated with the use of the MAOIs which can be a problem if not managed carefully. To understand why one type of anti-depressant might be used or preferred over another, it is necessary to understand the difference in their action and where norepinephrine comes from.

Norepinephrine is continuously synthesized from the amino acid tyrosine. Much of it is inactivated by the enzyme monoamine oxidase so that norepinephrine levels are maintained in balance. When the action of the MAO enzyme is inhibited by the use of an MAOI, the norepinephrine supply is increased. The nerve impulse can then release more norepinephrine. This is the basic principle behind the actions of the MAOI's. By increasing the amount of norepinephrine available at the synapse and, therefore, at the receptor sites, the mood state is altered and depression is lifted. In other words, the natural, balanced levels of norepinephrine are interfered with by using a drug which inhibits the action of an enzyme which serves to inactivate norepinephrine. The system then has more norepinephrine supplied and the depleted state known as depression is changed chemically.

What of the behavioral changes associated with his bio-chemically altered mood state? For most people who take MAOIs and who are able to go through the side effects and remain constant with the diet restrictions, there is a dramatic change in behavior. When the depression is lifted, much of the anxiety and panic reactions characteristic of Agoraphobia are also affected for the better. At this point, the application of the principles of behavior modification and exposure therapy are important. Because his depression is lifted, the Agoraphobic has more energy and interest in moving forward toward normal activities. It is necessary that this new, good feeling be channeled in the directions that will insure behavioral success. The ideal situation exists for combining the best forms of treatment presently known, bio-chemical intervention to combat depression and behavior modification to change learned habits. Current research indicates that the MAOIs are especially effective in dealing with the symptoms of Agoraphobia. The drugs, while acting on the depression as described here, also have a strong effect in reducing panic and anxiety attacks. Studies have shown that once the depression is reduced and the threat of panic has subsided, Agoraphobics respond extremely well to in vivo experiences and the return to near normal lives.

The other large class of anti-depressant drugs which should be discussed are the tricyclic anti-depressants (TCAs).

Their bio-chemical action is different from that of the MAOIs. The tricyclics work by blocking reuptake of norepinephrine, whereas the MAOIs act by inhibiting MAO. The blocking of reuptake functions in the following way:

When a nerve impulse releases norepinephrine to the synapse for a receptor response, there are several physiologic processes which take part in limiting the duration of the action of the norepinephrine. One of these processes is called reuptake. This occurs when some of the norepinephrine is taken back into the nerve-end pool from the synapse. By acting to inhibit or delay this reuptake, the tricyclic anti-depressants (TCAs) help to prolong or intensify the action of norepinephrine at the synapse. This has the effect of providing additional norepinephrine and other depression fighting chemicals to the brain. This is obviously a different type of bio-chemical process to overcome depression and to counteract the deficient levels of norepinephrine. As in the case of the MAOIs, it is vital to combine this therapy with behavioral change therapy. In some cases the lessening of Agoraphobic symptoms of fear, avoidance, anxiety and panic is not so dramatic or so quickly achieved when TCAs are used as when MAOIs are used. However, regardless of the type of anti-depressant drug therapy, a combination of techniques is always the best for the Agoraphobic.

It has been observed that there is sometimes a great difference in response between those who take the TCAs and those who take the MAOIs. Why this is the case and why some Agoraphobics get a good, positive reaction from tricyclic anti-depressants, while others require the MAOIs for noticeable results, is not fully understood at this time. Differences in individual chemistry, resulting in different levels of depression, as well as many other complex reasons may be postulated. What is important is that there *are* drugs available to help in combating the symptoms of depression and Agoraphobia. There are proven good results from using these medications along with other therapies discussed. Why, then, are Agoraphobics reluctant to take advantage of this availability?

The question of the reluctance of the average Agoraphobic to avail himself of the help of any therapy can be answered partially by considering his personality and his lifestyle.

The few studies which have been conducted of the personality configuration of Agoraphobics show them to share certain traits. Whether these common traits are due to the effects of Agoraphobia or whether certain types of personalities develop depressions and often Agoraphobic symptoms is a moot point at this time. In analyzing the studies, and from my personal experience in knowing dozens of Agoraphobics and in working with many of them in group and individual cases, it is clear to me that there are, indeed, important personality factors which are shared and some of these traits are significant when considering resistance to drug therapy.

A prevailing mental and emotional set for most Agoraphobics is fear. Fear is a constant companion and is the first reaction to nearly every situation, particulary if it presents something new or different. Given this attitude, the prospect of taking a medication over which he has no control once it is ingested, is fear provoking. The fear is chiefly the fear of loss of control of himself and his feelings. It has been noted that Agoraphobics are hyper-sensitive to their surroundings. They are also acutely aware of personal bodily feelings. Since there are many somatic changes which occur when fear, anxiety, and panic are constantly being felt, the prospect of experiencing new or changed bodily sensations which may accompany drug therapy, adds a new dimension to the sensitivity already present. Living with Agoraphobia means tuning in on every subtle physical feeling, being aware of temperature changes, noise levels, activities without and within which may pose a threat and activate the fear response. The side effects of many drugs is always an unknown for each individual taking them. The Agoraphobic who is hyper-responsive is fearful that he will develop all the

111

side effects, lose the control that he carefully cultivates, and succumb to his worst fears.

An examination of the concept of control is important here. If a single statement were needed to accurately describe an Agoraphobic, it would be that he is a person overwhelmed by fear, but constantly striving for control. Control of his feelings, his environment, his life situation; control of the small, safe world he has left. It is the factor of control which often confuses both professionals and non-professionals about the nature of Agoraphobia. Because the Agoraphobic is so facile at appearing normal, so used to hiding his feelings, he may fool those around him as to his real feelings. He is "hanging on" but no one knows it. If he appears somewhat anxious to his doctor, a tranquilizer will be prescribed. This is counter-productive for both the depression and the Agoraphobia. The depressed mood, the apathy, the reduction in physical and psychic energy which accompany the use of tranquilizers, removes control from the Agoraphobic and places it into a pill. Negative experience with tranquilizers is another reason Agoraphobics are reluctant to try drug therapy. They have been conditioned to expect a negative result from taking medication, so their natural hesitancy to try something new has been reinforced.

An additional personal characteristic of Agoraphobics which is important is that of impatience. Because they are so used to rushing through experiences to have them over or to avoid the effects of their own anxiety and panic, they have little patience. Since the anti-depressant drugs require a certain period of time before they become effective and also because the various side effects persist for some time, many Agoraphobics are ill-prepared psychologically to accept medication. There is a characteristic tendency to handle the idea of pills much as they handle their lives; to rush through things and to need instant results.

In trying to understand the Agoraphobic and his seeming indifference toward drug therapy, it is important to remember that his lifestyle for some period of time (perhaps his entire life) has been filled with frustration. Usually he has tried many routes toward wellness and found each in turn has defeated him. Besides his fears, he has become cynical and feels no one can really help him. Medicine has failed to understand his symptoms, and psychiatry has often mis-diagnosed him. So rather than try another approach to his problem, he prefers his familiar way of life—miserable as it may be.

There is one interesting paradox to be considered which is also a part of the Agoraphobic personality and life-style. That paradox involves hypochondria. While his attitude toward medication for his Agoraphobia is often intractable, at the same time he is often so aware of every body change and sensation that he presents the picture of a typical hypochondriac. If he can visit a doctor's office, he is usually there because of some minor or imagined illness. He will usually take whatever prescription is offered and sometimes is, in fact, ill due to the stress he lives under. While he will use medication to relieve his bodily problems, he cannot tolerate the possibility of using a drug for his emotional difficulties.

Some of the burden for changing this picture of the Agoraphobic and his resistance to medication must be assumed by the Agoraphobic himself. But the helping professions of psychology and psychiatry need to make a special effort in the area of patient education. This means not only educating the patients they see in their offices as to the duration of side effects, what reactions should be cause for concern and which are to be expected, but also for the Agoraphobic especially, it is vital that a complete explanation is given and assurances that the doctor is available for any questions should it be necessary. It is also incumbent upon the professions to make themselves knowledgeable concerning the relationship between depression and Agoraphobia and the use of the anti-depressant drugs in their treatment. Professionals, patients and families must be educated to the fact that drugs may be risky but the trade-off in the change in chemistry that helps bring about a change in behavior is worth the slight risk and discomfort of side effects. Agoraphobics must learn to trust their medication and their relearning and then trust themselves.

Some of the latest statistics state that one in one-hundred-sixty people suffer from Agoraphobia. If that number is anywhere near the case, Agoraphobia is far from an isolated, neurotic phenomenon. For those who have it and for those whose lives touch others who have it, it is past time for ignoring its ravages. It is time for caring, for knowledge, and for help.